ancient wine, new wineskins

ancient wine, new wineskins

The Lord's Supper in Old Testament Perspective

Jon L. Berquist

Chalice Press
St. Louis, Missouri

Library of Congress Cataloging-in-Publication Data

Berquist, Jon L.
    Ancient wine, new wineskins : the Lord's Supper in Old Testament perspective.
Includes bibliographical references and index.
1. Lord's Supper. 2. Worship in the Bible. I. Title
BV825.2.B47 1991   234'.163   91-25310
ISBN 0-8272-0019-6

For Terry,
who always believes
and whose belief always inspires.

acknowledgments

Throughout the course of this past year, many persons have joined with me in the process of thinking these thoughts. My thanks go to Phillips Graduate Seminary for bringing many of these people together and inviting me into their midst.

In the summer of 1990, I was involved with one of the groups preparing for the General Assembly of the Christian Church (Disciples of Christ) in 1991, to be held in Tulsa, Oklahoma, centering on the theme of communion. When one of our denominational leaders asked politely what things I might be able to contribute to the church's discussions of communion, another person answered first: "Of course, an Old Testament professor won't have anything to say about communion!" On that day, the idea for this book began. Inadvertently dropped seeds sometimes grow, and for those offhand remarks I am honestly grateful.

Throughout this project, David Polk of Chalice Press has pressed, prodded, challenged, and invigorated me. This relationship has gone from the formal tones of business and academics to the warmth of friendship, and in the process he has strengthened this book beyond what I thought possible.

Many friends have listened to me talk about communion, and I especially appreciate East Side Christian Church, Harvard Avenue Christian Church, and Memorial Drive United Methodist Church, all of Tulsa, and Hurst Christian Church, of Hurst, Texas, for inviting me to speak on these issues. There is no end to my thanks for those who have read early drafts of these chapters and have offered critique: Terry Berquist, Loren Crow, Peggy Dean, Lauren Odell-Scott, Leslie Penrose, and Linda Reis. My friends, your words echo in these pages, and your caring reverberates in my soul.

Terry Berquist was with me before this book, and now that the long hours of this project have come to their close, she's still speaking to me. In between, she did whatever was needed to bring this book to birth. I owe her much, much more than these pages.

contents

1

---

introduction

Today's Christianity exists in many forms. We are Catholic, Protestant, and Orthodox; conservative and liberal; mainline and renewal; denominations, brotherhoods, nondenominational, interdenominational, independent, and union; liturgical and free; high church and low church; traditional, radical, evangelical, charismatic, feminist; churches and small groups; and innumerable other categories, all of which contribute to the wonderful—and sometimes daunting—diversity that is Christ's church. Each part of the church looks a bit different from the rest, though we share some remarkable family resemblances. Walking into another congregation means experiencing something similar to our own customs and habits, but it means coming across something different, whether that is new, fresh, challenging, threatening, disturbing, or empowering. Yet we still feel some sort of common bonds, or at least we acknowledge that we should.

Although a diversity of forms and structures can benefit the church, we also divide into factions. We are a fractured church. We define ourselves a thousand different ways and then pit "us" against "them." The "others" don't do things right, or they don't believe the right doctrines, or they don't organize their church structures in the right way, or they let the wrong kind of people in, or they leave out people they shouldn't, or their morals are bad, or their worship is corrupt. Before long, our differences become the only things we see, which is probably a sure sign that we have stopped looking at the similarities, at the core of our faith in Jesus Christ, that should keep us together.[1]

Communion offers a way to solve our alienation from each other. That is hardly an original statement. It dates back to Paul's letter to the Corinthians, or it may even be older than that. Communion was an important common expression of the one Christian faith in the one God for the early followers, as it was for the Christians of the Restoration movement on the United States' frontier, some two centuries ago.[2] In recent years, ecumenical discussions have recognized that communion must be a place where we can meet in common, if any sort of meeting at all will be possible.[3] Communion calls all Christians, regardless of their differences, to remember the one Lord; we all trace our faith back to that Last Supper.

Communion is a decidedly Christian affair. It speaks to the core of who we are in Christ Jesus. The bread of Jesus' body is the enduring, empowering spiritual food that the church today so deeply needs. The cup that reminds of Jesus' shed blood forms the lifeblood of all churches today. The centrality of the table speaks of how we come together at table, each from our own places in life to one core where many gather as one church. Communion also asserts the true right of Jesus Christ to host the meal in praise of God, with us in attendance as invited guests, instead of as lords of our own separate tables. Communion embodies much of who we are as the Christian church.

Perhaps the unity and the diversity of the Christian church finds its clearest expression in communion. In wine and grape

---

[1] Jon L. Berquist, "Malachi: Laity in an Age of Pluralism," *Quarterly Review,* Vol. 11 (forthcoming, 1991).

[2] For a history of this movement, see Lester G. McAllister and William E. Tucker, *Journey in Faith: A History of the Christian Church (Disciples of Christ)* (St. Louis: Bethany Press, 1975). For comments on the practice of eucharist in this tradition, see also Keith Watkins, *The Breaking of Bread: An Approach to Worship for the Christian Churches (Disciples of Christ)* (St. Louis: Bethany Press, 1966); and Keith Watkins, *The Feast of Joy: The Lord's Supper in Free Churches* (St. Louis: Bethany Press, 1977).

[3] See *Baptism, Eucharist and Ministry,* Faith and Order Paper 111 (Geneva: World Council of Churches, 1982). A very helpful volume, containing prayers and liturgies from a wide variety of Christian traditions, is Max Thurian and Geoffrey Wainwright, eds., *Baptism and Eucharist: Ecumenical Convergence in Celebration,* Faith and Order Paper 117 (Geneva: World Council of Churches, 1983).

juice, in wafer and tablet and loaf, in prayer rail and brass tray, in all the variations we find our many differences given concrete form. It is sad to remember that churches have split over the issues of how to perform communion. These differences divide us, but the fact that we all continue to gather around communion tables, conducting services that are remarkably similar, is an important expression of who we are—the one church of God that Christ intended. The differences should not divide, because the similarities are so striking.[4] Communion has the power to bring us back together at the one table of Jesus, even against our petty strugglings for the positions that define our own righteousness.

The church of today faces other problems as well. The church has distanced itself from the world. We have invented forms of spirituality that have so little to do with the rest of our lives. Church services become a way of escape from the world, as we recognize every time we talk about worship as a moment of quiet or as a time set apart from the busyness and clamor of the world. We have made faith mean nothing more than a set of beliefs that can be encapsulated into words, whether they are neat confessions or complicated systematic theologies. When religion becomes nothing more than words, then the rest of life goes untouched by our spirituality. Too easily we forget that faith and action are inseparable. We must answer the call to be in the midst of the world, where Christ is. Only then will we have a faith that is relevant, meaningful, and capable of attracting others. Faith is a way of living life, not a set of creeds or doctrines. When the church distances itself from the world, then Christians distance their faith from the rest of their lives, robbing faith of its greatest power to bring meaning to human existence.

Not only are we divided among ourselves and unattached to our world, but we alienate ourselves from our own past. Throughout the history of the Christian church, there has been a disturbing tendency to accept the New Testament as somehow more central, more vital, or more spiritual than the Old Testament. Although the ancient church declared this to be heresy, the tendency persists, but the cost is great. The Old Testament

---

[4] Dennis E. Smith and Hal E. Taussig, *Many Tables: The Eucharist in the New Testament and Liturgy Today* (Philadelphia: Trinity Press International, 1990).

contains many riches that are relevant for modern Christian faith. Its stories tell of faithful persons in many different situations, some with amazing parallels to our own journeys. The Old Testament helps establish moral standards, giving voice to ideals that still have relevance. The prophets share visions of the way we should live in God's world and call even us to make these dreams come true. The wisdom writers speculate about God's nature and show us patterns of thought from which we can still learn. Through these and other matters, the Old Testament presents a rich tradition of faith that is thoroughly grounded in day-to-day existence. We cannot afford to attempt a faith that does not build upon the foundations of the whole Bible.

Since communion lies at the heart of our shared experience as church and as Christians, it seems then, a sensible place to start to reclaim our most ancient heritage. Of course, the Old Testament mentions nothing of practices of communion. The church traces communion back to Jesus' last supper,which is described near the conclusions of the Gospels. But communion was a new practice that built on ancient foundations, and those building blocks are found in the Old Testament.

Communion is an act in which the church has much invested. All the most valuable theological ideas of our common faith coalesce in the cup and the bread. Many of these notions, if not all of them, are themes that go far beyond communion: God's costly caring for people, God's choice of workers within the world, God's salvific empowering of persons for that work, and so many other ideas. These notions mingle in the cup, but they flow in many other directions as well. The Old Testament themes show us one dimension to these ideas, helping us recognize a richer variety within the biblical expressions of communion, so we can appreciate and appropriate the fullness of our faith.

We are doing nothing new here. We only travel down the paths that others have walked before.[5] By focusing on Old Testament ideas that relate to the themes of communion, we are doing what the early church might well have done. The earliest church thought in terms informed by their Hebrew Bible

---

[5]See F. Gavin, *The Jewish Antecedents of the Christian Sacraments* (London: SPCK, 1928; reprinted New York: KTAV Publishing House, 1969); and Harvey H. Guthrie, Jr., *Theology as Thanksgiving: From Israel's Psalms to the Church's Eucharist* (New York: Seabury Press, 1981). For a Roman Catholic view of these issues, see Tad W. Guzie, *Jesus and the Eucharist* (New York: Paulist Press, 1974).

heritage (as is clear from the widespread New Testament use of Old Testament citations, allusions, and categories of thought) and their understandings of communion expressed the influences of this previous religious heritage. The Old Testament provided the vocabulary in which early Christians and the New Testament writers talked about their experiences and their faith. By learning more of that ancient vocabulary of images for ourselves, we can join more fully in the earliest understandings of Christ and communion.

History is vital to an understanding of the Bible, both Old and New Testaments. Past events occur within the context of other past events, and so history is vital to understanding how all these events relate to each other. Therefore, this book will touch on many issues within biblical history. However, historical connections are not the focus. Instead, the meaning behind the events receives the greatest attention. Many of these biblical stories seem almost beyond belief. If we attempt to verify their facticity using historical means, we gain nothing. If we understand their meaning and look within the stories to meet the God of whom all these texts speak, then we gain immensely. Through all of this, our gaze falls upon the way the stories are told and the faith that they embody. The goal of this book is not to determine precisely what happened in the past, but to discover theological resources for our life in the present.

Communion as a historical event was a unique phenomenon. Though connected to the ancient Jewish Passover tradition and to other practices and thoughts of first-century Judaism, communion is fundamentally its own institution. Therefore, the stories we hear and tell are not accounts of historical causation. All of these Old Testament ideas did not automatically combine into a new practice that we call communion. Instead, Jesus began a new practice, and the early church struggled to understand it, just as we continue that struggle. The comprehension is so difficult because communion is so packed with meaning; no amount of theologizing can say everything that can be said. But when the early Christians talked about communion, they used Old Testament language and reflected on their other stories of faith, the stories that are recorded in our Old Testament. So we join in reflecting on communion and on the Old Testament, and we find an amazing number of connections. Our minds wander throughout the history of God's people and we find one God who deserves our worship and our thinking.

The themes treated in this book fall into three broad categories. Firstly, the elements themselves receive consideration. Communion consists of simple items, the bread and the cup, combined in a way that is reminiscent of the ancient Jewish Passover. These elements make up communion, in one sense. The second section of the book examines the people. Who are the people who gather at the table? What kind of people should we be when we meet there? Into what kind of community will the table transform us? Lastly, theological issues come to the forefront. What are the ideas about God that undergird all of these practices? Who is the God whom we meet at the table? In this fashion, the book centers on the communion table, looking first at the meal, then at the people who partake, and then at the God who invites.

Elements

If asked to describe communion, we would probably start with the elements: bread and wine. These elements conjure up in one's mind many Old Testament connections. Manna falls from the skies to feed the wandering Israelites in the wilderness. They are thankful to God for a while, but then their grumbling starts again. They don't want the same dry food every day, every week, every year. But this manna gives them sustenance in a simple, boring way. Communion, too, is a consistent meal. The content never changes. One congregation will probably use the same brands for the elements for decades. Of course, the elements are not themselves the saving factor; they symbolize much more important things. Still, we fall quickly into the habit of allowing no variety for this fixed meal, just as was the case with manna.

If there are historical connections to be made between the early church's communion and the Old Testament, then certainly they connect at Passover. This Jewish holiday was the one that Jesus and the disciples were celebrating when Jesus added a few words to the standard Passover liturgy, giving us communion's words of institution. Passover, then, is a rich resource for understanding our own communion traditions.

Bread and cup each deserve separate attention. These elements symbolize so many parts of our faith. Through looking at Old Testament images of bread and wine, two ideas come to the forefront. Bread represents God's sustaining and healing. Bread restores life in both mundane and miraculous ways. Our daily bread gives life for a new day, along with new possibilities for how to live that life. At certain special times, bread can give life when life's end was thought to be near. Bread empowers the weak and brings all of God's people into the right kind of life. The cup of wine in the Old Testament is often a severe image. God brings judgment through cups of wine. In this way, God punishes the exploitative nations of the world and even makes Israel drink the cup of God's wrath. Several New Testament passages understand communion's cup of wine in much the same way. The cup of communion discerns and judges our deepest selves, also desiring to purify.

Community

The elements await us at the table, but the event is not communion until the community gathers at that table. Communion brings God's people together and makes them one. It can be a joyous celebration when all of God's people join together in unity. Many biblical texts embody the notions of celebration and unity, including prophetic visions in Isaiah, Zechariah, and Revelation. Communion is not just a meal; it is a feast thrown by the Creator of the universe to which all are invited. When the invitation is accepted, a party ensues.

At the table, the community begins its transformation. Because God invites all people, those at the table must share a common concern for each other. In our world, this means a concern for economics. How can some people participate in God's own feast when others in the world are starving? All are called to the table, and it becomes our responsibility to make sure that all can arrive safely. This is part of the care for the other guests that God expects when we come to this party.

Morality is another issue that arises around the table. This is not just any party; it is God's party and we are expected to live by God's standards. The table marks us as followers of the God who hosts the party and of the Christ who began it. We should act like followers. The world calls us to many different parties, but we choose God's communion table, and that choice makes us morally different. The table transforms us into God's true community.

Theology

Theological discussions about communion have too often dealt with technical terms such as transubstantiation and consubstantiation, which are theories about how the elements are related to Jesus Christ. But communion expresses many more ideas about God. One of those ideas is covenant. God and humanity are partners in an agreement, in which God offers instruction about life and faithful care and humans return faithful service. God's goal is the salvation of the world, and God will stop at nothing to achieve it. The partnership means that God and people work together for the same goals, and those goals remind us of themselves when we gather at the table.

The church has also explained communion in terms of atonement and sacrifice. Because Jesus died as a sacrifice for our sins, we are forgiven and cleansed. The Old Testament contains a richly developed understanding of sacrifices and atonement, and a close examination of these themes aids greatly our attempts to comprehend Jesus through communion. God works earnestly, through the death of Jesus as well as through communion and many other ways, to eradicate sin from the world. The communion table invites us to join in this work and brings forgiveness to ourselves and to the rest of the world.

If there is one event that communion commemorates, it is Jesus. Communion reminds us of Jesus' life, death, and resurrection. All must be considered together. Death and life join at the table. Communion can bring lively, vital meaning to all of life, even to death. Also, communion remembers the God who can bring life where there is death. Resurrection and meaningful death are both results of meeting God, as we do at the table.

Ancient Wine, New Wineskins

The struggle to find relevance in the Old Testament is hardly new; Jesus preached from the Old Testament and argued over its significance for life and faith. Once, Jesus offered a metaphor to understand the process:

Neither is new wine poured into old wineskins; otherwise, the wineskins burst, and the wine is spilled, and the skins are destroyed; but new wine is poured into fresh wineskins, and so both are preserved.

Matthew 9:17[6]

This common-sense saying explains the problems of combining the new and the old. This is a problem familiar to every person and every church. Growth must continue; there must always be new wine. But how can it relate to what has already happened, to the old traditions that are best known and loved? If new and old come together in the wrong fashion, it violates the older things and ruins what is new.

This book attempts to put ancient wine into new wineskins. Wine that is well-aged will not split new skins, since the new skins are supple and resilient. The use of aged wine allows for the best of the old to be preserved and enjoyed in new ways and in new forms. Both old and new are honored.[7] In this case, the ancient traditions of the Old Testament are put into the new forms of the New Testament and the early church's communion. These ancient biblical traditions and our communion traditions, many of which have been in place for decades and centuries, are presented in a new light so that fresh possibilities can be found. With ancient wine and new wineskins, the best of communion is yet to come!

---

[6] All scriptural quotations throughout the book are the author's translations.

[7] One might compare Luke's version of this saying (5:37–39), which ends, "No one who has drunk aged wine desires the new, but says, 'The old is better.'"

I

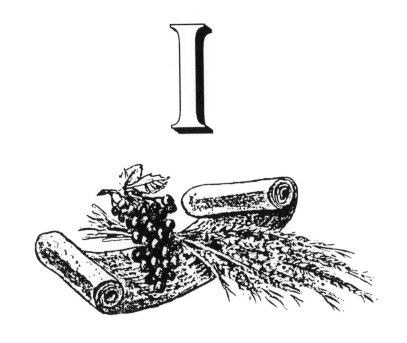

---

elements

2

manna
and
passover

On the first day of Unleavened Bread the disciples came toward Jesus, saying, "Where do you wish that we prepare for you to eat the Passover?" He said, "Go into the city to a certain one, and say to him, 'The Teacher says, My time is near; I will carry out the Passover at your house with my disciples.'" The disciples did as Jesus had directed them, and they prepared the Passover.

Matthew 26:17–19

The history of communion connects this central Christian sacrament with another religious observance, the Passover, also called the feast of Unleavened Bread. Passover was a Jewish festival that was centuries old by the time that Jesus entered Jerusalem to celebrate it with his disciples. The roots of Passover extend back in time to the Exodus. Israel's memories of its first Passover tell the story of the flight from Egypt after God's repeated plagues convinced Pharaoh to let the people go. The holiday and festival of Passover commemorated this formative event in the identity and faith of the Israelite people. It became a symbol for everything that they were. The annual Passover meals were a way of marking the passage of time. It seemed that significant things were bound to happen at Passover.

Jesus' disciples were Jews by ethnicity and by faith, as Jesus was himself. As faithful Jews, there was never any question in their minds that they would celebrate the Passover in the traditional way. Since they were a traveling company, they would observe Passover together, instead of breaking the group apart so that each could go worship with their respective families. There is little indication that there was much advance planning among the disciples. Almost at the last minute, they all start doing what comes naturally to get ready for this annual event. They rent a room in someone's house so that they can have the traditional meal there. They buy and bring together the accustomed foods, cooked and assembled in the traditional ways. The stage is set for a very typical Passover.

Certainly, this Passover meal shared by Jesus and the twelve disciples begins as a common one. The usual Jewish prayers would have been said at the appointed times through-out the meal. The prayer for liberation from their oppressors, Roman and otherwise, would have been on their lips and in their minds, as they remembered together the liberation from slavery that God had provided for their ancestors in Egypt.

Within the liturgy of Passover, there were many symbolic foods, eaten in a certain order with standard prayers of blessing and thanksgiving associated with each. During one of the blessings of the bread, Jesus blessed it in the usual way, and then added a sentence for the disciples: "Take; eat; this is my body" (Matthew 26:26). Throughout the meal, the participants drink from four cups of wine. When taking one of these four cups, Jesus gave the usual prayer of thanksgiving to the God who makes the vine grow and give forth its fruit. Then, Jesus added more: "Drink from it, all of you; for this is my blood of the covenant, which is poured out for many for the removal of sins" (Matthew 26:27).

Jesus took the traditional Passover meal and added just a few words. The meaning of all the other Passover celebrations was still present in this meal that Jesus asserted would be his last supper on earth. With a few additions to the Passover meal, the early church declared that it possessed a new celebration. They called this new religious observance by many names over time; some of the more familiar terms are eucharist, mass, Lord's Supper, and communion. Though the church has increasingly removed this sacrament from its roots as a variation on the Jewish Passover, elements of those early meanings still reside in this central Christian act of remembrance.[1] Two images from the Passover

---

[1] In this century, numerous liturgical reform movements have called for a return to earlier forms and Jewish roots. For a Roman Catholic example, see The Bishop's Committee on the Liturgy, *The*

celebration must be recalled in order to understand more fully the communion of the early church: the manna of the wilderness and the blood of the Passover.

Manna

The Exodus brought salvation to the Hebrews who had been slaves in Egypt. God raised a unique leader, Moses, who challenged Pharaoh and unified the people to lead them out of Egypt, with the Egyptian royal military forces right behind them. At the Sea of Reeds, just when Pharaoh's forces thought that they had reached the place for a decisive confrontation, a miraculous crossing of that sea saved the former slaves from wholesale slaughter. From there, the Hebrews thought, their path to the promised land, a land flowing with milk and honey, would be free and clear. Moses and the rest of the Israelites broke forth in song to celebrate their remarkable salvation, while Miriam directed the music and led the women in a dance.

Let me sing for Yahweh,
for this is extremely wonderful:
horse and its rider God has thrown into the sea.
Yahweh is my strength and might,
and God has become salvation for me;
this is my God, whom I will praise,
my ancestors' God, whom I will exalt.

Who is like you among the gods, O Yahweh?
Who is like you, majestic in holiness,
awesomely praiseworthy, doing wonders?
You stretched out your right hand,
earth swallowed them.
In your steadfast love you led
        the people whom you purchased;
you guided them by your strength
        to your holy abode.

You brought them and planted them
        on the mountain of your own heritage,

Mystery of Faith: A Study of the Structural Elements of the Order of Mass (Washington, DC: Federation of Diocesan Liturgical Commissions, 1981), especially pages 71, 78.

the place that you made your tribe, O Yahweh,
the sanctuary, my Lord, that your hands
        have established.
Yahweh will reign forever and ever.
                        Exodus 15:1–2, 11–13, 17–18

The other side of the Sea of Reeds was no promised land,
however. Moses' band found there a wilderness that was wild
and untamed. This deserted land was not at all hospitable to
human life. Food was scarce, as was water. Without even the
basic necessities of human life, the Israelites were hard pressed
to see how their current status was any better than slavery in
Egypt. Within six weeks, their supplies were completely gone.
Their mood then turned even more sour:

> The whole congregation of the Israelites grumbled about
> Moses and Aaron in the wilderness. The Israelites said to
> them, "If only we had died by Yahweh's power in the
> country of Egypt, when we sat by the meat pots, when we
> ate bread to our satisfaction! But you brought us out into
> this wilderness to kill this whole assembly with hunger."
>   Exodus 16:2–3

The situation was nearly out of control. The people's complaints against their human leaders now even involve God.
These disenchanted Israelites would prefer death at God's
hand, presumably through the plagues that had devastated
Egypt, rather than the life of freedom and hunger that was
now their lot in the desert. With fond remembrance, they
think about the large stew-pots that were set out among the
slaves in Egypt, into which each could dip bread in the broth,
though they would not have been allowed to eat the stew itself.
The Egyptians ate the meat; the slaves sponged up the broth. At
least there was plenty of bread, and at least there was something
to give the bread flavor. In the desert, there was nothing—only
empty stomachs—and these people would prefer slavery to
that.

The Gift of Manna

Many Christians consider the God of the Old Testament to
be hard-hearted and stubborn, a God of wrath and anger who is

quick to punish and slow to love.[2] If that were true, then one would expect God now to destroy the Israelites. God's own people prefer Pharaoh's security to God's freedom, even after God has saved them. With frightening frankness, the people dare to test God. They embody the most amazing ingratitude and accuse God's chosen one, Moses, of evil intentions in trying to kill the whole people with hunger. The people have affronted God, and we can guess the risks involved with such an affront. As one expects, God is quick to speak in response to the people's complaint. Immediately, God sends a message to Moses:

> "I am going to make bread rain down from heaven for you, and the people shall go out each day and gather some for that day. In that way I will test them, whether they will walk within my instruction or not. But on the sixth day, when they prepare what they bring, it will be twice as much as they gather each day."
>
> Exodus 16:4–5

God is quick to speak promises of love and provision, not judgment and curse. Of course, God's permanent intention of removing sin from the world is still present; God intends to see whether or not the people truly will follow. But in the meantime, God will give the people their daily bread and will forgive their iniquities of rejecting God and complaining about God's servant. God even provides double on the day before Sabbath, so that the people do not have to work by collecting the bread on the Sabbath itself. God's desire is for people to obey, and God does everything possible to make that possible. God even provides food for the people, in realization that starving persons rarely make good religious followers—a lesson that the church of today is slow in learning as we debate evangelism and social

---

[2] Too quickly forgotten or misinterpreted are texts like Exodus 34:6–7: "Yahweh, Yahweh, a God of compassion and mercy, slow to anger, and abundant in loyalty and truth, preserving loyalty for thousands, taking away iniquity and sin, who will in no way consider innocent the guilty, pursuing the iniquity of the ancestors upon the children and the grandchildren, to the third and the fourth generations." The ending of such a statement of faith is harsh, but it must be interpreted along with the rest of the verse. God is loving, but God is also serious about having a world without sin, for the benefit of the creatures whom God loves so much.

mission, thinking at times that the two are not both necessary in God's plans.

Just as God is quick to speak love and provision, Moses and Aaron are quick to pass on the good news to the people:

> In the evening you shall know that Yahweh brought you out from the country of Egypt, and in the morning you shall see the glory of Yahweh, who has heard your complaining against Yahweh. What are we, that you complain against us?
>
> Exodus 16:6–7

Moses and Aaron tell the people that God will provide, and the people await proof in silent expectation. The story gives us no clue what they thought would happen, whether they believed or they doubted. Instead, the story simply moves to the results: God was faithful and did provide, as was promised. This was not just food; it was a visible and public demonstration of the glory of God.

Moses and Aaron realize the true nature of this situation. Though the people have complained to Moses about his leadership, Moses and Aaron know that their human leadership is not the true issue behind the complaints. Instead, the people are unhappy with God. In admitting this publicly, Moses and Aaron have committed a rare admission for the leaders of any human group. They have admitted their own lack of control. They have brought the people out of Egypt, but they cannot provide food. "What are we, that you complain against us?" They know that they are helpless and that the people know that their human leaders are helpless to solve the situation.[3] Only God can bring food into the empty wilderness. Thus the emphasis of

---

[3] Moses does not maintain this proper perspective on his own power throughout his time as Israel's leader. His sin occurs at Meribah, where Moses called forth water of a rock by hitting it with his staff. This was done successfully on God's command in Exodus 17:1–7; Moses admitted the limits of his own power and thus there was no sin. The situation was repeated in Numbers 20:2–13. That time, God commands the same event, but Moses now has words to say to the people while striking the rock: "Listen, rebels! From this rock shall we bring forth water for you?" (Numbers 20:10). The water came forth to cure the people of their thirst, because God still provided for those in need, but God chastised Moses for words that attributed to Moses, not to God, the ability to provide for the people.

this part of the story is on the provision of God; the human leaders, Moses and Aaron, fade almost entirely into the background for the following miraculous scene.

> In the morning there was a layer of dew all around the camp. When the layer of dew lifted, upon the surface of the wilderness there was a tiny crisp something, as tiny as frost on the ground. When the Israelites saw it, they said to one another, "What is it?" because they did not know what it was. Moses said to them, "It is the bread that Yahweh is giving for you to eat."
>
> Exodus 16:13b–15

Again, the miraculous nature of the gift points to the God who provides the people with what they need. The community's human leadership is not the source of the gift; it is God alone, and Moses' job is to deny the credit and to tell the people that *God* provides.

This scene represents miraculous divine action. However, it also shows the human and the humorous. Moses has told the people what to expect; they should be ready for a miracle. Furthermore, the Israelites had seen plenty of God's miracles, from the Egyptian plagues to the parting of the Sea of Reeds. Over and over again, they had seen what God could do. They should have known that God was unpredictable and uncontrollable, and that their requests for bread and for provision would be answered, but not necessarily in the ways that they would have thought. They should have expected the unexpected.

On the other hand, these people have not lost their capacity to be amazed. Even though they have seen wonders on a regular basis, they can still be shocked. They retain a keen sensitivity. They have also maintained a sense of humor that comes through when one reads the story carefully. All of Israel awakes early in the morning, in excited anticipation for the wonderful meal they expect to find waiting for them outside the camp. They rush to find what's there, chattering with each other along the way, wondering together what this meal from God might be. Is it some sort of ambrosia, a miraculous food of the gods? Will it make them stronger than any other nation ever has been, so that perhaps they can turn back and conquer Egypt and live there forever with others as their slaves? Will it be a valuable delicacy, perhaps one that can be sold worldwide at a high price, like caviar or truffles or champagne, so that they can become the wealthiest nation on earth? Will it taste so good as to send all of Israel into culinary ecstasy? Will they become a people of abundance because of this gift? All these questions fall from their frantic lips as they rush to see what God has provided for them.

Unexplainable Manna

Then they reach the clearing just as the morning light dawns, and they begin to see. But truthfully, they don't see much of anything. Sure, there's some dew on the ground, but there's nothing else: no lavish meals, no dainty delicacies, no robust foods. They wait, maybe thinking that something may yet appear. The murmuring and grumbling begins again, as some people question whether this God will ever be reliable enough to provide adequately for the people. Again, their minds turn back to the abundant bread of Egypt, even though they were given only the tiniest fraction of what that wealthy nation had to offer.

Then the dew starts to melt, and someone notices that the food is *under* the dew. Of course, any food that can hide under dew is not much food at all, but it's still food. At least, it *might* be food. It's hard to tell at a distance. Someone moves closer and scoops up a handful of the stuff. It's white and grainy. It's in a thin layer all over the ground; it might take a lot of back-breaking scooping in order to gather enough for any sort of meal, let alone to collect enough for a day's worth for a good-sized family. Then it would still have to be baked and prepared.

Someone else shouts, "What is it?" Soon, the question is echoed throughout the crowd. "What is it?" No one knows. No one has ever seen it or anything like it before. They've never talked to anyone who had seen anything like it. No one even knew what to name it. Eventually, they started calling it *man-hu* or manna, which is Hebrew for "what's-it." This type of food was totally unexpected by the people. They didn't even have the vocabulary to deal with it.

Uncontrollable Manna

Moses is the only one who can answer the question about the white flakes from the sky. He does not provide them, however, with a vocabulary word to fit the definition that the people have just learned from experience. Instead, Moses talks about the source of the *man-hu* and the instructions for using it. The question "What is it?" is never answered; Moses tells who sent it and what the people should do with it.

> "This is what Yahweh commands: 'Gather it, each as much as you will eat, an omer per person according to the number of persons, each giving to those in one's own tent.'" The Israelites did so, and they gathered, some more, some less. When they measured it into omers, those who gathered more had nothing left, and those who gathered less did not lack; each gathered as much as each would eat.
>
> Exodus 16:16–18

This strange manna becomes stranger still. God commands through Moses that each person should take an omer, about two quarts.[4] That should be enough for a one day supply. In other words, everyone should have exactly as much as they need to eat. Some of the Israelites are industrious. They gather more than their fair share, but when they get back to the camp, they have only one omer each. No matter how hard they try or what their motives are, they can't get any more than that. Perhaps they were trying to gather extra manna, so that it could be hoarded or sold. If so, God has prevented any such manipulation right from the start, because no one gets more than they need, no matter how hard they work for it. On the other hand, those who are too weak to gather a full day's supply are not forgotten. The God who provides for the nation of Israel provides enough for each person, regardless of abilities or efforts. All should eat; but none should have an abundance that might give them advantage or control.

Thus the provision of manna is a miracle in another way. Not only are the people blessed by God's gift of free food, but there is no possible way to misappropriate or misuse the gift. Greed or power cannot pervert this gift, nor can weakness or inability lessen any person's right to benefit from it. It is a gift for all and is shared equally by all, whether the people want to share

---

[4] William G. Dever, "Weights and Measures," in *Harper's Bible Dictionary*, ed. by Paul J. Achtemeier (San Francisco: Harper and Row, 1985), p. 1131.

equally or not. For a moment, it seems absolutely impossible to mismanage this miracle.[5] But that moment is sadly brief.

> Moses said to them, "Let no one leave it over until morning." But they did not listen to Moses. When some people left some of it until morning, it grew worms and spoiled. Moses was angry with them. They gathered it every morning, as much as each would eat; but when the sun was hot, it melted.
>
> Exodus 16:19–21

It appears that God had thought about every way that the manna could be misused. No one can go without enough and no one can collect more than they can use. But the people find a way to damage the free gift of God. A few of the Israelites do not trust the miracle. They have gone hungry in the wilderness for a long time, and they have become wary. They are not about to eat all of their newfound bounty in one day, because they were not convinced that there would be any the next day. Just to be on the safe side, they stored some of the first day's manna, in case they didn't get any the next day. Instead of trusting in the God whose caring provision had already been demonstrated just that morning, they wanted security. Instead of God's unexpected good favor toward the Israelites, they wanted predictability. But their desires for predictability and security resulted in worms feeding on the decaying manna. The attempts at control ruined the gift of God. Without the trust, there was nothing left for them to eat. God can provide for the people, even for the greedy people and for the unproductive people, but the untrusting, controlling people find no benefit in God. For them there is no manna the next day—only worms and rot.

The people had to eat the manna. This was not some simplistic "clean your plate and be thankful for what you've got because other people have even less" morality. It was much more than that. The manna was a true gift of God, and true gifts require active acceptance in order to be effective. Those who

---

[5] The phrase echoes Bernard Brandon Scott, *Hear Then the Parable: A Commentary on the Parables of Jesus* (Minneapolis: Fortress Press, 1989), pp. 127-140. His reference is to Luke 12:16–20, the parable of the man whose unexpected death prevents enjoyment of his newly built barn full of hoarded food. Hoarding is a violation of God's principles and thus a mismanagement of any miracle.

wished control were rejecting God's gift of bread for today by preferring to guarantee that they would have bread for tomorrow. The impulse toward control had destroyed some people's knowledge of what to do with bread from heaven. They did not even know what to do with a free gift, because their minds were blinded by their attempts to mismanage the miracle. They rejected God's gift and received what they deserved—nothing edible.

If human tendencies to bungle God's free gifts can never be forgotten, then neither can God's gracious providing be underestimated. On the next morning, sunrise revealed another fresh supply of manna for everyone. God did not carry a grudge against those who wanted to hoard the bread. It would have served those control-minded persons right if they did not receive their daily supply of manna, so that they would be forced to go hungry and to think about their mistake. But God provides. The second day's free gift of manna is just like the first day's miracle. God refuses to punish the greedy in an attempt to make them change their ways. Instead, God chooses to love them into changing, with the hope that daily, regular demonstrations of God's loving care might drive away the fears that cause the greedy to stockpile their goods in futility. So God provides the second day just as the first, and so the week goes on in divine regularity of provision.

The Sufficiency of Manna

This went on for five days, with all the people receiving each day exactly enough to meet their needs. The manna allowed no surpluses and no shortages, so everyone received God's provision equally. For five days, things were precisely the same every day, and the people began to believe that God would always take care of them with manna. Then came the sixth day, and things changed—just as Moses had told them beforehand.

On the sixth day, they gathered twice as much bread, two omers each. When all the leaders of the congregation came together, they told Moses, and he said to them, "This is what Yahweh said: 'Tomorrow is for solemn rest, a holy sabbath to Yahweh. Bake what you normally bake and boil what you normally boil, and all that remains leave alone to keep until the morning.'" So they left it alone until the morning, as Moses commanded them. It did not spoil, and there were no worms in it. Moses said, "Eat it today, for today is a sabbath for Yahweh. Today you will not find it in the field. Six days you shall gather it; on the seventh day, which is sabbath, there will be none there." But on the seventh day some of the people went out to gather; they found none.

Exodus 16:22–27

On the sixth morning, the rules change again. The white flakes are twice as deep over the ground around the Israelites' camp. The people step out on that bright morning, amazed at the sight of extra manna. Now there is surplus and plenty! They rush out to the fields to gather what they can. It takes them longer than usual to finish the backbreaking labor of scooping these abundant flakes from the ground, but the thoughts of what they can do with the extra makes the work worthwhile to them. Maybe they can find someone to trade with them, so that they can get some other sort of food to go along with their manna. Perhaps they can afford to settle down and live a more comfortable life with their newly enhanced income from God. Maybe their only thoughts are on their own soon-to-be-full bellies. The possibilities seem endless to them as they gather up their bounty.

With excitement the Israelites come back into the camp, having scooped up all that they can carry. They measure their large quantities and find that each had two omers, instead of the one omer that they had gathered every other day. They are rich! Their salaries have doubled! God has given them *twice* their daily bread!

All the Israelites' leaders rushed to tell Moses the good news. After all, Moses not only had brought the people out of Egypt, but also had endured the people's grumbling and complaining about his leadership. Now, Moses had really come through for them; he deserved some gratitude from the usually ungrateful people. Moses heard the news and smiled. He said, "Good! I'm glad you collected extra today. Just be sure not to eat it; save it to eat tomorrow when you need to participate in God's Sabbath." The leaders would have been in shock. They would have stared at Moses in utter amazement. How could he talk like that? Doesn't he see the possibilities for advancement that this extra manna represents?

Moses rejected the ideas of control and profit and instead spoke in the language of faith and worship. The manna is God's gift and thus should be used in the fashion that God intends. God did not design manna as fodder for economic growth, but as food to bring life to the people. In response to the God who gives, the people give thanks for those gifts. This means that the Israelites should observe a day of rest on the seventh day, just as God rested on the seventh day of creation. There will be no manna distributed from the sky on the seventh day, because God rests on that day. Because God rests, the people should also rest.

God's gift of rest and God's gift of food are not contradictory. Because heaven's bakeries are shut down on the seventh day, then there is double on the sixth. God's provision for the people never ceases and nothing gets in its way. On the other hand, the Israelites must be very careful not to eat the seventh day's bread on the sixth. Nothing will stop them from it, but they must remember that there is no food on the seventh day. The sudden bounty on the sixth day is not for immediate consumption, or for hoarding and selling. Instead, it is only intended to keep the daily provision for the people.

Some of the people complained about this, if they were at all like us. They had seen what had happened when someone tried to store manna overnight. It became fit only for the worms that were already eating it. How could they be expected to keep half of it overnight, knowing what it would look like at the dawn of the seventh day? But such was God's commandment through Moses, and such was what the people did. The morning of the seventh day came, and then they found out that not only was the sixth day's manna twice as much, but it was also a special recipe that did not sour in twenty-four hours. Instead, it had a longer expiration period. Those who had been patient and who had trusted God found that they had enough to eat on the seventh day; those who had hoarded the double portion of manna in the stomachs experienced no food, only indigestion from overeating.

In the face of this miraculous provision that matched the call of God to observe the Sabbath, the seventh day came, and most of the people found that there was enough good food in their houses to meet their needs for the day, though a few people never learned the lesson properly. Those few ate their fill in their homes, and then went out to the fields to look for more. Some people never learn. Outside the camp, they found nothing.

Perhaps at last they started to believe that God really was faithful as well as compassionate in providing for the people, but such was unlikely. At every step along the way during the first week of God's manna, some of the people had misunderstood. Although God's provision gave the Israelites food to eat in reliable and sufficient quantities, some always mistrusted God and acted on their own ideas instead of living through faith. Manna is many things, then: a food, a sign of miraculous and sufficient provision, a lesson in God's faith, and a chance for people to choose that faith. If the people reject faith and live by their own ideas, they will find that such action produces no true benefit for anyone.

The Memory of Manna

The manna was God's reliable provision for forty years, as Israel wandered through the wilderness on their way to the promised land. Despite the depths of care shown through the provision of the manna, God knew that there would be a day when the people would reach that promised land, and then the manna would end. In preparation for that day, God commanded Moses to remember what was happening.

> Moses said, "This is what Yahweh commanded: 'Take a full omer of it to keep for your future generations, so that they can see the bread that I gave you to eat in the wilderness, when I brought you out of the country of Egypt.'" Then Moses said to Aaron, "Take a single jar, and put in it a full omer of manna. Set it before Yahweh, to keep for your future generations." Just as Yahweh commanded Moses, so Aaron set it before the congregation to keep it.
>
> Exodus 16:32–34

The ark of the covenant became the resting place for the last omer of manna. This omer was a very special recipe—it never went bad, even for centuries. Manna was provision, but it was also a lesson of faith, and that lesson lasted long after the need for bread from heaven was gone.

The Lesson of Manna

Manna taught the people about God on a daily basis. Every morning, six days a week, the gathering of the manna offered hands-on experience with God's miracles. Slowly, throughout the forty years in the wilderness, perhaps the Israelites learned their lesson.

Manna is a gift that God gave to the people. It was not something that the people earned through their good deeds. Not only did the Israelites not deserve the manna, but they were asking for punishment when they complained to God that the departure from Egypt was the wrong thing to do. The people rejected God's plan for their lives, but God started to provide for them. God knew that hungry people rarely learn about God except through food given to them, and people who have already starved to death never learn anything new about God at all. In order for God to keep educating the people, provision was required, and it took the form of manna.

The manna was available in nearly endless amounts, but the sheer vastness of the white flakes on the field was never the point of the lesson. Instead, manna taught the people that God was deeply concerned with each one of them. Not only was there enough manna for the whole nation; but there was exactly enough for each individual. No one went without; no one hoarded the manna to keep others from eating their fair share. God's grace knows no bounds, but the amount that it takes for each person is exactly measured to be precisely sufficient for all of each person's needs.

The goal of the manna was the sustenance of daily life. It was not God's intention to give the people a supernatural strength-enhancing food that would create a race of muscle-bound warriors who could take the promised land from its inhabitants without any loss of life. God did not intend the manna to increase the wealth of the nation so that they could become rich and powerful among the nations of the earth. Instead, the manna was provided for the everyday needs of the people. It was a mundane food, not a delicacy. Manna was simple food, so all the people could simply live.[6]

Manna was inexplicable. No scientists could figure out what happened; even today's scientists make only poor guesses

---

[6] Perhaps these images also connect with the church's traditions of fasting. Through fasting, we recognize that God is sufficient for us, and this can also help us reflect on those persons without sufficient food.

when faced with explaining this miracle.[7] But explanations were never important; one did not have to understand the manna in order to eat it. Manna was not meant to be explained but to be experienced.

Likewise, manna was uncontrollable. Of course, many of the Israelites tried to control it. They tried to hoard it, to preserve it, to gather more than their share of it, to be lazy and go without it, to get twice their share on the sixth day, and to get another share on the seventh. All of these attempts at control failed. The bread from heaven could never be under human control. Since it could not be controlled, it could not be used for economic benefit or for any other person's desires. It was only good for one thing: keeping God's people alive and whole as a community. Any other uses were futile.

Manna was God's sufficient, uncontrollable, unexplainable gift of life and provision to the Israelites for forty memorable years in the wilderness. It was a strong lesson in grace and in faith for those Israelites who experienced it. The lesson continues today, when Christians gather around the table in worship of a God whose gifts are sufficient for human needs. God is still unexplainably gracious and uncontrollably independent. God still provides the bread of life that teaches faith. Though the name of God's bread has changed from manna to communion, God is still the same.

Passover

Manna is the story of God's gracious provision for the people, but the story of the flight from Egypt through the wilderness to the promised land does not begin with manna. The story begins with Passover, where God shows a very different kind of provision for the Israelites. In the events of the Passover, God demonstrates the cost of such care and provision.

----

[7] A leading explanation is that manna was the honeylike secretions of the bush form of the tamarisk. These secretions came out overnight and dried quickly; within a day, ants would eat it all if it was not collected. See Loren D. Crow, "Plants of the Bible," in *Mercer Dictionary of the Bible,* ed. by Watson E. Mills (Macon, Georgia: Mercer University Press, 1990)pp. 692–696. Although such scientific musings are helpful in our envisioning of the situation, the story's point does not depend on the nature of the manna, but rather on the reasons behind its presence and the understanding of God embodied in these texts.

The First Passover

The story of the first Passover really begins long before that earth-shaking event in Egypt. Its roots are in the family stories of Genesis. These stories tell about Abraham and Sarah, Isaac and Rebekah, and Jacob and his two wives, Leah and Rachel. Jacob, whose name became Israel, had twelve sons, including his favorite, Joseph. Joseph's older brothers hated him because of his dreams and his favorite status, so they hatched a plot against Joseph. As a result, Joseph was sold into slavery, and eventually was taken to Egypt. There Joseph rose from being a slave to the position at the Pharaoh's right hand. When Jacob and the rest of the family were suffering from a drought and a famine that nearly killed them, they went to Egypt seeking aid, and were reunited with Joseph, who was now in a position to help them. Jacob's whole family moved to Egypt, where there was food.[8]

Years passed as the Israelites lived in safety and peace in Egypt, but then the political climate changed. The earlier stories of Joseph's well-deserved favor from the Pharaoh had been forgotten. A new Pharaoh was not willing to give them any privilege, but instead enslaved all of Jacob's descendants. Then the enslavement turned to genocide and the Egyptian government ordered the death of a whole generation of Israelites. There was one remarkable exception—an infant who was taken in by Pharaoh's daughter and raised as an Egyptian, though he was secretly an Israelite. This boy grew up in the court as Pharaoh's grandson and he was called by an Egyptian name, Moses.[9]

As befitting one of Pharaoh's grandsons, Moses was trained for a career in governmental service. While on the job observing Pharaoh's subjects, Moses noticed a case of injustice: an Egyptian overseer beating a Hebrew slave. Moses violated Egyptian law by murdering the unjust overseer. When his deed became known, Moses fled Egypt in order to escape his adopted grandfather's wrath. Moses wandered into Midian,

---

[8] This story can be found in Genesis 37—50.

[9] For a lively discussion of these Exodus stories, see Carol A. Newsom, "Retelling the Story of the Exodus: Homiletical Resources for the Season after Pentecost," *Quarterly Review*, Vol. 7, No. 2 (Summer 1987), pp. 71-100.

where he befriended the family of a priest named Jethro, who gave Moses his daughter, Zipporah, as wife. Moses' second career was in Midian as one of his father-in-law's shepherds. In the meantime, the Pharaoh died and was replaced by one of his sons, who would have been one of Moses' uncles.

One afternoon, while Moses was keeping watch over the sheep, he noticed a bush that burned strangely. When he went over to see what was happening, he heard a voice, which turned out to be the voice of God:

> I have watched closely the misery of my people, who are in Egypt. I have heard their cry as a result of their taskmasters. Truly, I know their pain, so I will come down to rescue them from Egypt, and to bring them up from that country to a good and wide country, to a country flowing with milk and honey, to the place of the Canaanites, the Hittites, the Amorites, the Perizzites, the Hivites, and the Jebusites. Now has the cry of the Israelites come to me. I have also watched the Egyptians oppress them. So come, I will send you to Pharaoh to bring my people, the Israelites, out of Egypt.
>
> Exodus 3:7–10

The struggle of Moses against Pharaoh to gain the release of God's people from Egyptian slavery is one of the great confrontations of the Bible. God's intention to bring the people out of oppression into "a country flowing with milk and honey" is not accomplished easily. The confrontation starts on a relatively calm note:

> Afterward, Moses and Aaron went and said to Pharaoh, "Thus says Yahweh, the God of Israel, 'Send my people, and they will celebrate a festival to me in the wilderness.'" Pharaoh said, "Who is Yahweh, that I should obey by sending Israel? I do not know Yahweh and I will not send Israel."
>
> Exodus 5:1–2

Pharaoh's resolve to keep the people in slavery toughens and the oppression of the Israelites increases. Small miracles, such as the change of a staff to a snake, do not change Pharaoh's mind. Then God initiates a series of destructive assaults upon all the nation of Egypt, in order to force Pharaoh's hand. These assaults included turning all water into blood and killing the rivers; unleashing frogs, gnats, and flies throughout the nation;

spreading infectious disease and skin sores; sending thunder and lethal hail; bringing locusts to swarm; creating a thick darkness throughout the land (Exodus 7—11). Although these made Pharaoh willing to negotiate for the Israelite release, after each disaster Pharaoh was just as resolved to keep the Israelites as Egypt's slaves. The ninth disaster, darkness, angered Pharaoh so much that he refused to continue talking with Moses.

> Pharaoh said to him, "Go away from me! Take care that you never again see my face, for on the day you see my face you shall die." Moses said, "Just as you say! I will never see your face again."
>
> Exodus 10:28–29

God and Moses discuss the problem, and then Moses announces God's decision for one final plague. Pharaoh has raised the stakes; God will call Egypt's bluff.

> Moses said, "Thus says Yahweh: About midnight I will go out into the middle of Egypt, and each firstborn in the country of Egypt shall die, from the firstborn of Pharaoh who sits on his throne to the firstborn of the female slave who is behind the handmill, and all the firstborn of the livestock. Then there will be a loud cry in the whole country of Egypt, such as has never been or ever will be again."
>
> Exodus 11:4–6

Through nine plagues, God has tried to free the Israelites with only little cost. Now God contemplates the truly terrifying. It is difficult for us to defend God's actions in this scene of the Passover story.[10] The cost of the salvation for the Israelites is staggering. A few other factors must be kept in mind, however. Moses has repeated the message to Pharaoh on God's behalf more than ten times already. God responds now with death in order to save the lives of the numerous nation of the Israelites.

---

[10]Truly, our modern viewpoints can hardly comprehend the violent actions that this story attributes to God. For ancient peoples, however, the situation was quite different. The Exodus texts are part of Israel's belief that God would act against God's enemies, who were also the enemies of God's people. Within such a system of thought, God's violent actions here are salvation, and would never suggest any theological problem at all. Instead, these ancient peoples might scratch their heads in bewilderment at the God of passivity and blindness to injustice that we often prefer.

Even after this severe provocation, God's action is in smaller proportion when compared to Egypt's actions against the Israelites. The former Pharaoh attempted to kill every male child of the Israelites (Exodus 1:15–22); God refuses that degree of violence. If there is any lesson that can be drawn from this horrible tale at all, it is that God will purchase freedom from oppression even at the price of doing what God has already forbidden. The God who has endowed humanity with moral choice, in all its glories and pains, faces the same problems, and at times will perform costly deeds to eradicate injustice.

At midnight death came to Egypt. At dawn the cries of anguish rose to the heavens, but Israel had already gone. Passover had begun.

God commanded the people to make a solemn observance of this horrible event. Each year at this time, all the Israelites were to remember what had happened and the price at which God purchased their salvation. The observance involves seven days without work and without leaven. Instead, the days are concentrated on reflection about the exit from Egypt. Passover remembrance focuses on the blood of the lamb that has purchased their salvation.

> Moses called all the elders of Israel and said to them, "Go, take sheep for your families, and slaughter a lamb for the passover. Then take a brush made of herb, dip it in the blood in the basin, and touch the lintel and the two doorposts with the blood from the basin. You may not go out through the door of your house until morning. Yahweh will cross over to strike Egypt. If God sees blood upon the lintel and upon the two doorposts, Yahweh will pass over the door and will not allow the destroyer to enter your houses to strike it. You shall keep this as a continuing obligation for you and your children. When you enter the country that Yahweh gives you, just as God has said, you shall keep this service of worship. If your children ask you, 'What is this service of worship for you?' then say, 'It is the passover sacrifice to Yahweh, who passed over the houses of the Israelites in Egypt, when God struck Egypt and rescued our houses.'" And the people bowed down and worshiped. The Israelites went and did just as Yahweh commanded Moses and Aaron.
>
> Exodus 12:21–28

Each year, the people remember God's salvation at Passover. A slaughtered lamb gives its blood so that death may pass over the Israelite houses instead of passing through them, as death comes through the Egyptian households. Salvation has its cost. The Egyptians pay dearly with the loss of their firstborn. The Israelites have already paid through generations of slavery. Each year, the cost of a slaughtered lamb is paid to remember the greater prices paid before.

Passover begins as a most solemn observance, remembering the cost at which God saved the Israelites. Throughout the history of the people, however, Passover became a joyous time, celebrated through a meal of lamb and through the wine that flows generously then. There is both solemnity and rejoicing when the people remember their salvation.

The wine of communion carries that sense of joy and solemnity. There is marvelous rejoicing in that celebration of God's salvation that occurs during communion. The wine that reminds us of Christ's gift assures us of our own salvation. But when the words of institution echo in our minds, the images of Jesus' death come to us almost unbidden. Passover's wine reminds the Israelites of blood; the lamb reminds them of God's sacrifice of the firstborn. In the same way, communion's wine stirs thoughts of Jesus' blood, the slaughtered lamb, and the firstborn of God. Solemnity is not far away when we think of communion, but the joy of God's salvation, purchased at great price, should also be close at hand.

Passover and Wilderness

Passover reminds us of communion's cups of wine, helping us think of the cost at which God saves all people. After the Passover came the wilderness, when God saved in a different way. The marvelous, miraculous salvation through plagues and through the crossing of the Sea of Reeds had passed and had brought the people into a wilderness, not into the promised land. In the wilderness, God's salvation takes the form of white flakes underneath the morning dew. In this manna, the people discover that God cares about them and sustains their daily life in uncontrollable, unexplainable ways. Both Passover wine and wilderness manna speak about God's deliverance; thus, they belong together so that we can hear the full range of God's love and salvation.

Bread and wine belong together, because both communicate God's salvation in unique and complementary ways. The cost of deliverance and the constant care of salvation are both part of God's work with humanity, and it is the fullness of that work that the church today remembers and celebrates in the bread and wine of communion.

3

the bread
that
restores

Manna, like the bread of communion, is a gift from God. Together with the wine of communion, the bread is the gift of God for the people of God. We may confess that all the food we eat is a gift from God, but there is a difference. Our usual food brings us strength but also has a cost; we must put forth work to grow it or money to buy it. Manna was a *direct* gift from God. All the Israelites had to do was collect it. It was not earned food, but an unearned gift—true grace.

God's bread brings healing and restoration to the people of God. Manna met a specific need of hunger, while at the same time expressing God's care. The gift of manna also addressed another need. The people had a complaint against God that was deeper than the food shortage: they wished to go back to Egypt. With the gift of manna, God removed their excuse and gave them the strength to go forward, not backward to Egypt.

Manna was empowerment, healing, and restoration. It fed body and soul alike. Healing and restoration were also characteristics of the Sabbath, where we turn next to investigate bread's healing and restorative powers.

Bread and Sabbath

Sabbath as Restoration

Christians often think of the Sabbath as a restriction. Certainly there were those in Jesus' time that understood

Sabbath in that way. Most of us are more familiar with the New Testament stories where Jesus confronts the Pharisees and others over the right to live decently on the Sabbath, so it is likely that we forget some of the original impact of the Sabbath in Jewish thought.[1]

Sabbath was the seventh day of the week, the traditional day of rest. Of the Ten Commandments, the fourth concerns the Sabbath:

> Remember the day of rest (Sabbath), thus keeping it holy. Six days should you labor, and do all your work. The seventh day is rest (Sabbath) for Yahweh your God. You should not do any work—you, your son and your daughter, your male and female slave, your beasts, and your resident alien. For in six days, Yahweh made the sky and the earth, the sea and all that is in it. On the seventh day, God relaxed. Therefore, Yahweh blessed the day of rest and consecrated it.
>
> Exodus 20: 8–11

Sabbath is not just a tradition or a custom; it is a commandment by God for all people. God's followers are commanded to keep the Sabbath day holy by refraining from work. Sabbath is a day of resting and restoring one's strength. It is specified that it is for everyone, rich and poor alike. Sabbath is the only commandment that is explicitly applied to all categories of society. This time of rest is for everyone.

The Sabbath commandment is also the only one that is traced back to the very beginning. These commandments start with the reminder that God is the one who has brought the people out of Egypt (Exodus 20:2–3). The salvation experienced by the people when God brought them out of Egypt is the context for the other commandments, but the Sabbath is more basic than that. Its roots precede God's salvation in the Exodus, coming from creation itself.[2]

---

[1] See the discussion of Sabbath in Walter Harrelson, *The Ten Commandments and Human Rights*, Overtures to Biblical Theology 8 (Philadelphia: Fortress Press, 1980), pp. 79-92.

[2] However, the version of the Ten Commandments in Deuteronomy 5 gives a different motivation for the Sabbath commandment. In that list, God's salvation in the Exodus is the reason for Sabbath rest.

At the conclusion of the Priestly telling of the creation story, we hear:

> On the seventh day, God finished the work that God did. God rested on the seventh day from all the work that God did. Then God blessed the seventh day and consecrated it, because on it God rested from all the work that God had created to do.
>
> Genesis 2:2–3

According to this Priestly writer, Sabbath is the climax of God's creative work. The commandment for humanity to observe the Sabbath is not explicitly stated here. Instead, there is simply the statement that God rested on the Sabbath, blessing it and setting it apart. People should then, by nature, follow God's example and set this seventh day apart for rest. The need for rest is in no sense an arbitrary whim by a lawgiving God; rather, it is a necessity built into the very nature of creation. From the beginning, according to the biblical story, the rhythm of seventh-day rest was known to the people and was recognized as a gift from God.

Since both Sabbath and manna were understood as the free gifts of a gracious God, it is no surprise what God does on the first Sabbath after the manna's arrival. Before starting the manna, God had explained what would happen: "On the sixth day, when they prepare what they bring, it will be twice as much as they gather each day" (Exodus 16:5). Through Moses, God had told the people what to expect. Provisions had already been made. The need for Sabbath rest was recognized and it would have been ludicrous for God to have given the gift of manna without remembering and honoring the prior gift of Sabbath. Although it was not surprising what God did to care for the people by providing two gifts of restoration in manna and in the Sabbath, neither was it surprising what the people did, since they were the same sort of people we are today. They wondered. They doubted. They looked for some way to take advantage. So some went out to gather on the Sabbath. They were afraid that they would not have enough if they did not go out to collect more. They were concerned that after only a few days of having daily bread, they suddenly had none.

God was patient, though, and reminded the people that the previous day's gathering was sufficient. The sixth day's food was enough for two days, so that the Sabbath could remain a day of rest. Both manna and Sabbath were God's gifts to restore the people; neither gift would contradict the other.[3]

Bread for Sabbath

Manna taught the people that God's gift of bread did not contradict the gift of rest on the Sabbath, since both manna and Sabbath were gifts for the purpose of restoration. A different bread taught the people that bread was *meant* for the Sabbath.

The book of Leviticus details how Aaron, along with Moses' help, followed God's directions to form a priesthood for the people. Part of the priestly system was a provision for bread to restore the strength of the priests.

> Take flour and bake it into twelve loaves; two-tenths of an ephah shall be in each loaf. Then place them in two rows, six per row, on the golden table before Yahweh. Put with the two rows pure frankincense. This will be for the bread as a memorial, as an offering by fire for Yahweh. Each sabbath day, Aaron shall arrange them before Yahweh on behalf of the Israelites, as a covenant forever. They shall be for Aaron and his descendants, who will eat them in the sanctuary, because they are holy portions for him from the offerings by fire for Yahweh, a continual obligation.
>
> Leviticus 24:5–9

This bread, called showbread in older translations, was intended to strengthen and restore the priests. Each week a new batch was placed by the altar, then the priests ate the old batch of bread, which had been sitting there for a full week, filling with the smoke of the altar and of the frankincense.

Whereas manna had been intended to strengthen the people of Israel physically, this priests' bread from the altar was hardly a major portion of the priests' diet. It was not so much sustenance as symbol. This bread had been in the presence of the altar and had been filled with the smoke that was understood to be an embodiment of God's presence. The priests ate

---

[3] For a fuller discussion of Sabbath and manna, see Walter Brueggemann, *Finally Comes the Poet: Daring Speech for Proclamation* (Minneapolis: Fortress Press, 1989), pp. 90-99.

the bread to partake of God's presence, which would sustain not so much their bodies but their ability to function as God's priests throughout the week. The eating of this holy bread sanctified the priests for their ministry that lay ahead and restored them to the special close relationship with God that made their work possible. It was powerful bread that brought the priests closer to God.

Not for Priests Only

This bread that sat on the altar before God was meant for the priests, but in one case it was eaten by nonpriests. Before David became king, there was a time when King Saul wanted to kill him. Saul sent part of the army to chase David, causing him to flee for his life. Exhausted and hungry, David and his friends came to the city of Nob, looking for food and rest.

> David came to Nob, to Ahimelech the priest. Ahimelech came trembling to meet David, and said to him, "Why are you alone, and no one with you?" David said to Ahimelech the priest, "The king has commanded me something, saying to me, 'Let no one know a thing of the matter about which I have sent you and commanded you.' I have informed the young men concerning a certain place. Now, what have you at hand? Give me five loaves of bread, or whatever can be found." The priest answered David, "I have no regular bread at hand, only holy bread." …So the priest gave him the holy bread, because there was no bread there except the bread of the Presence, which is removed from before Yahweh in order to put hot bread there on the day it is taken away.
>
> 1 Samuel 21:1–4a, 6

David and his friends needed food, so they asked for the holy bread from the altar, if that was all that could be found to eat. The priest Ahimelech agreed to give them the holy bread. What a scandal! A ragtag bunch wandered into a local sanctuary and asked for the bread from the altar to eat, and the priest said yes! The bread intended for priests went to homeless, wandering renegades. The further one looks, the greater the scandal becomes. David, the future king, has lied to get the bread. He had claimed to be on a secret mission from King Saul when, in reality, he was on the run from the king. The scandal was so blatant that it was still talked about in Jesus' day (Mark 2:23–28). But the story in 1 Samuel makes one disturbing fact clear: Despite the regulation that the bread was for the priests, despite David's lying about his situation, the priest Ahimelech was right to give the holy bread to David and his friends. Giving the bread may have been illegal and scandalous, but bread is intended to meet the need of hunger, as well as the priests' need of sanctification.

Jesus and Healing

When Jesus talked about how needs of hunger, healing, and restoration must be met by God's servants, he referred to this story of David and the holy bread.

> One sabbath, Jesus was passing by the grainfields; and as they made their way his disciples began to pluck ears of grain. The Pharisees said to him, "Look, why are they doing what is not permitted on the sabbath?" Jesus said to them, "Have you never read what David did when he and those with him had need and were hungry, how he entered the house of God (when Abiathar was high priest) and ate the bread of the Presence, which is not lawful to eat except for priests, and he gave some to those with him?" Then he said to them, "The sabbath was made for people, not people for the sabbath; so the Son of Man is lord also of the sabbath."

> Once again, Jesus entered the synagogue. There was a man with a withered hand. They watched whether Jesus would heal him on the sabbath, so that they could accuse him. He said to the man with the withered hand, "Come forward." Then he said to them, "Is it permitted on the sabbath to do good or to do harm, to save life or to kill?" But they were silent. Jesus looked around at them with anger, grieved at their hardness of heart, and said to the man, "Stretch out your hand." He stretched it out, and his hand was restored.

> Mark 2:23—3:5

This pair of connected stories from Jesus' early ministry shows Jesus' combination of these themes of bread, Sabbath, and restoration. God's gifts of bread and grain are for restoration, just as the Sabbath is human restoration. Thus, it is right to pick grain for food on the Sabbath, since both are God's gifts. It may not be legal, but it is right. In the same way, it is right to cause life and to do good on the Sabbath, such as in the healing of the man with the withered hand. This is how Jesus understood his healing: it was an act of restoration, which fit with God's larger purposes for Sabbath.

Sabbath—and the bread that comes on Sabbath—is not just for devotion. Acts of piety are appropriate for the Sabbath, but restoration and healing fit best with the true meaning of Sabbath. The same is true for bread. It is not just to strengthen faith and to sanctify the one who partakes; it is also to bring rest and restoration. This was the case with the bread of manna, with the bread of the altar eaten by the priests, with the bread taken from the altar by David and his companions, and with the grain picked from the field by Jesus and the disciples.

All of this is also true for the weekly bread of communion. This bread is a reminder of the true Sabbath. God provides the bread of the communion table just as God provided manna in the wilderness, as a free and gracious gift. It is a means of restoration for the people who partake. It is an act of devotion and sanctification, as Sabbath is and as the bread of God's Presence is. But the act of devotion should never obscure the true function of the communion bread in bringing healing and restoration. The bread is not holy because of what it *is*, but because of what it *does* in healing and restoring God's people.

Bread's Sufficiency

In the task of bringing healing and restoration to God's people, God's gift of bread is sufficient for God's purpose. It is commonplace to talk about the abundance of God's grace, but the bread of the Bible speaks of sufficiency. To our modern minds, so consumed by the struggle for affluence and abundance, sufficiency does not sound strong enough to describe God. But the amazing claim of bread is that it is sufficient—it is enough for God's purposes. It is not merely abundant; it is sufficient. Similar to the manna that fell from heaven, bread is enough to feed everyone exactly. Bread is neither extravagant, nor overabundant, but able to fulfill every need. The Israelites knew that an abundant supply of any food, even manna, would not go far to feed the multitudes reported in the Exodus and wilderness wandering stories. God's gift of manna is more than abundant; it is sufficient.

Abundance can be counted, and in our perverse human fashion it can even be controlled, manipulated, saved up, and parceled out.[4] We moderns turn abundance into distribution problems, with the result that people starve in the face of abundance, and even those who produce the food lose their farms to repossession. Manna is beyond abundance, beyond calculation, beyond control—beyond belief. It is sufficient. There is exactly enough to meet every need. In the same way, God's gift of bread is sufficient for life, for God's tasks, and for the building of community.

Sufficient for Life

The amazing sufficiency of bread for life becomes clear in one of the stories about Elijah's miracles. The prophet Elijah's ministry took place mostly during a period of drought in Israel; the dryness had caused a famine that threatened the lives of many.

> The word of Yahweh belonged to him, saying, "Get up and go to Zarephath, which belongs to Sidon, and live there. I have commanded a widow there to feed you." He rose and went to Zarephath and entered the gate of the town. A widow was there gathering wood. He called to her and said, "Please bring me a drop of water in a vessel, so I can drink." Once she went to fetch it, he called to her and said, "Please bring me a morsel of bread in your hand." But she said, "As Yahweh your God lives, I have nothing baked, only a handful of grain in a jar, and a drop of oil in a jug. I am gathering a couple of sticks, then I will go home and prepare it for myself and my son, so we can eat it, and then die." Elijah said to her, "Do not be afraid. Go and do just as you have said. Only, first make me a little cake of it and bring it to me, and then make something for yourself and your son after that. For thus says Yahweh, the God of Israel: The jar of grain will not be used up and the jug of oil will not fail until the day that

---

[4] See Brueggemann, *Finally Comes the Poet*, pp. 92–93.

Yahweh gives rain to the ground." She went and did just as Elijah said, and they ate for many days, he and she and her household. The jar of grain was not used up, neither did the jug of oil fail, just as Yahweh spoke through Elijah.

1 Kings 17:8–16

This story begins with a disaster waiting. Elijah makes his first prophetic proclamation to Ahab, the king of Israel: "As Yahweh the God of Israel lives, before whom I stand, there shall be neither dew nor rain these years, except by my word" (1 Kings 17:1). Then Elijah went to a brook where God fed him by way of ravens, but after the brook dried up, God sent Elijah to the widow of Zarephath. The reader can sense that things are going from bad to worse. In a time of drought and famine, the people who have the least are affected the most, and in ancient Israel this means that widows, the poorest element of society, become even poorer. Asking for food from a widow in a drought is nonsense—those who have nothing can give nothing.

At first, the reader's expectations are not disappointed. Elijah asks for water, as if widows have extra water to give. Imagine the look on her face at the temerity of such a request! Regardless of what was on her mind, she turned to fulfill the request. Then Elijah adds to his list of desires: "Perhaps you could bring a little something to eat with that, please. Just give me whatever you've got." At this remark, the widow speaks for the first time. She begins with an oath and continues to explain all of her problems. Note that she does not refuse the prophet, but she does make the situation clear. She is only a widow and starvation is close at hand. What does she have to give to anyone else? She will not even have her own life, or the life of her son, for much longer.

Elijah tells her to go forward with her plan and with his request. Then, he shares with her a word from God: "The jar of grain will not be used up and the jug of oil will not fail until the day that Yahweh gives rain to the ground." Once again, the bread from God is sufficient, but not abundant. There is no sudden surplus, no overflowing jars of grain or oil. There is, in fact, no more grain than what there was before. Instead, the grain that was almost gone somehow lasts for the widow, her son, and this stranger too.

The bread that comes in response to God's word is sufficient. Just like manna, it is uncontrollable—it cannot be stored or sold, since there is only enough for the moment. But there is always enough for the needs of those whose lives depend on it. When the story next tells of the widow's son growing sick to the point of death, it is almost anticlimactic that life will be given to the boy. The bread—and the word of God behind it—is sufficient to give life where life is needed.

Sufficient for the Task

Through bread, God gives the remarkable gift of life, but God also gives bread for more specific purposes. God's bread is sufficient for the tasks that God sets before people, as can be seen once more in Elijah's life. Elijah had just challenged the prophets of the Canaanite deity Baal, resulting in a marvelous victory on Mt. Carmel. Everyone who saw the spectacular miracles there confessed that the Lord was God, but not everyone in the kingdom was convinced; Queen Jezebel remained a Baal worshiper and she sent word to Elijah that she would have him killed, so he fled.

> Elijah walked into the wilderness for a day, and came and sat under a solitary broom tree. He asked that he might die: "It is enough, now, O Yahweh, take my life, for I am no better than my ancestors." He lay down and slept under the broom tree. Suddenly, an angel touched him and said to him, "Get up and eat." When he gazed around, at his head was a grilled cake and a jar of water. He ate and drank; then he lay down again. The angel of Yahweh came a second time, touched him, and said, "Get up and eat, or the travel will be too much for you." He got up, and ate and drank. He walked by the strength from that food forty days and forty nights, as far as Horeb, the mountain of God.
>
> 1 Kings 19:4–8

As this story of Elijah begins, it seems as if the themes are the same as that of the earlier story: God provides the bread that is sufficient for life. Certainly, Elijah was anxious for his own death. He had abandoned his hopes for life and was ready to give it up. Then God sends the angel to bring the bread that makes life possible, and the angel wakes Elijah up and commands him to eat. Again, this is the bread that restores life.

Then the plot twists. Elijah, endowed with new life because he has partaken of the bread of life, has returned to a peaceful sleep, but then the angel wakes him again. Elijah must have been surprised and confused. This prophet by now must have been accustomed to being fed in miraculous ways, but being awakened twice in one night by an angel bringing dinner was unusual even for him. Perhaps he had a quizzical look on his face. For some reason, the angel gives him a reason for the second command to eat. No reason was given the first time, and none was needed: it had been stated earlier in the story of Elijah that God's bread restores life and there was no need to mention it again. But something else is going on, and that something else requires an angelic explanation.

The angel commands Elijah, "Get up and eat, or the travel will be too much for you." The reason for the second portion of bread is the task at hand. Elijah wants to stop and die; the angelic visitation brings the bread that restores life and the second visit brings the bread that is sufficient for the task. Again, the bread is marvelously sufficient. On its strength alone Elijah can travel forty days and nights. God's gift of bread makes possible the completion of the task that has been given to Elijah.

Note that Elijah does not wish the task. Against so much of the theology on television today, God does not empower Elijah to do what he wants to do; God enables Elijah to do what God wants him to do. Bread is meant not to make one's own desires attainable, but to make God's plans possible. Elijah is given the strength to do what he does not want to do and to complete the journey and task from which he has been fleeing. The bread that is sufficient for the task brings strength and blessing, but it is heavily laced with challenge. One almost wonders if Elijah was tempted to choke on this thick bread of challenge, but he could certainly feel the strength that it gave him. After the restorative night of sleep and the healing, empowering twin meals, Elijah began his accomplishment of his divinely appointed task, thanks to the bread that was sufficient for that task.[5]

---

[5] The stories of Jesus' temptations in the wilderness provide a fascinating counterpoint. In the wilderness, Jesus fasted, though at the end angels ministered to him, just as they had ministered to Elijah. The bread that they gave Jesus strengthened him for the task of ministry. But Jesus makes another point about bread—bread by itself is not the true source of life. We live not by bread, but by God's word and grace. Bread can never be the end; it is only the means by which we find God. Such is true of communion as well.

Sufficient for Community

God's bread is sufficient for life and for the tasks that God gives. This bread is also sufficient to bring people together into the community. Bread, such as the bread of communion, brings all people together, even the most rejected. Such is the nature of God's bread, as shown so well in a story about four lepers in 2 Kings 7. These rejected lepers lived in the wilderness just outside the city of Samaria, the capital of the northern kingdom of Israel. Samaria was under siege at that time, being surrounded by the Arameans. The lepers were starving outside the city because of the famine, but they knew that they were not welcome inside the city of Samaria, either. The king and the other rulers of Samaria were the type of people who tried to control the supply of food, and the least desirable—such as the lepers—were the least likely to be given anything to eat. So these lepers, grasping at their last straw, went to the Aramean camp, looking for some charity—and some bread—at the hands of Israel's enemies.

To their surprise, they found the Aramean camp empty! Through a miracle, the Arameans had thought that they heard a great army, and they fled in panic, leaving all their supplies behind. The lepers went into the camp, plundering riches and especially the food, gorging themselves to their hearts' content. The bread restored their life and gave them strength; then they began to feel the challenge.

> They said to one another, "What we are doing is wrong. This is a day of good news. If we keep quiet and delay until the morning light, guilt will find us. We should go now and report this to the royal palace." When they arrived, they called to the gatekeepers of the city, and reported: "We went to the camp of Aram, but there was no one there, not even a sound of somone, except the horses tied up, the donkeys tied up, and the tents as they were." So the gatekeepers called out and reported it to the royal palace....Then the people went out, and plundered the camp of Aram. So a measure of choice meal was worth a shekel, and two measures of barley were worth a shekel, just as Yahweh had said.
>
> 2 Kings 7: 9–11, 16

God's bread went first to the most disadvantaged, after it had come through the hands of the despised enemy. This gift of bread subverts the standard expectations of how God works and who benefits from God's efforts in the world. Through a miracle, the lepers are given food to eat in amounts sufficient for life and for their task. But they do not have a task before they have the food, and they hear no angel voices to point out their task to them. Instead, they have only themselves—and an abandoned abundance of bread.

It is the bread itself that brings the conviction of a task. They are endowed with a sense of community. Though they had been thrown out of the city of Samaria, they still knew it as their home. They still felt some loyalty to those who had rejected them. So they felt that they could not sit and experience abundance by themselves. There was more than abundant food–there was the possibility of sufficiency for the whole city. The bread reminds them of the community from which they came.

Along with a sense of community, the bread restores in the four men a sense of identity. Before the bread, they were lepers, people who were pushed outside the city. They had been robbed of their identity. Perhaps it is better to say that they had been given a negative identity. They were defined by what they were *not*: They were not city residents, they were not safe people to be around, they were not worth having nearby. This was how the society defined them, thus it was how they identified themselves. Once the bread is in them, however, they begin to define themselves otherwise. Once more they see themselves as part of a larger group, the city of Samaria. They have communal responsibilities. They are restored by the bread, not just to life but especially to the community that had rejected them.

Because of the lepers, the people of Samaria were saved from the siege and from the famine that it had brought. The whole city experienced the miraculous sufficiency of God's bread. The disadvantaged and rejected lepers become the city's saviors; and the king, who should have been the one to save the city, cannot do anything but watch. At the end of the story, the people are fed, but the king's captain is killed, trampled by the crowds rushing out the city gate. Those who try to control the bread and who too narrowly define the community cannot stand in the raucous joy of God's salvation. Thus bread teaches about community in God's kingdom, where roles in society, such as leper and king's friend, are reversed. Bread, including the bread of communion, also reminds us that God draws the communal boundaries in amazingly inclusive ways. To do otherwise is to risk being trampled in the gate, like the king's captain.

Jesus and Bread

A discussion of bread and communion cannot be complete without reference to Jesus, who was the "bread that came down from heaven" (John 6:41). Like manna and all the other types of bread we have seen, Jesus intends restoration and Jesus' bread is sufficient for life, for the tasks before us, and for a new sense of identity and community. When Jesus touches the bread, all of these themes return to the scene.

Multiplication

As always before with God's bread in the Old Testament, Jesus' bread is miraculously sufficient for the needs of all those around, both the needs of body and the needs of spirit.

> As Jesus went ashore, he saw a large crowd. He had compassion for them and healed their sick. When it was evening, the disciples came to him, saying, "This place is empty, and the hour is already late. Send away the crowds, so that they may go into the villages and buy themselves food." Jesus said to them, "They have no need to go away; you give them something to eat." They replied, "We have nothing here except five loaves and two fish." And he said, "Bring them here to me." He urged the crowds to sit down on the grass. Taking the five loaves and the two fish, he looked up to heaven, and blessed and broke the loaves, and gave them to the disciples, and the disciples gave them to the crowds. All ate and were filled. They gathered the excess of broken pieces, twelve baskets full. Those who ate were about five thousand men, besides women and children.
>
> Matthew 14:14–21

On the surface, the sufficiency of Jesus' bread for life is clear. It is a miraculous sufficiency. Like the manna of old, it cannot be controlled. Matthew's presentation of this story offers a clear contrast between the disciples' suggestion that the people go into the villages and buy food and Jesus' command that the disciples provide the food. The disciples are thinking in terms of those who control bread. Food is to be found in the villages, the places of power over those who are on the outside. There the food is controlled by the rules of commerce, which determine who gets how much bread. Jesus thinks not in those terms of commerce and control but in the language of divine giving: "They have no need to go away; you *give* them something to eat." The disciples' response, like that of the widow of Zarephath, is a statement that comes before faith; it focuses on the nonabundance of bread. Jesus sees bread's potential sufficiency; from this insight stems the miracle of the feeding.

The disciples, however, are not slow-witted about this. They hear Jesus' words and understand. Perhaps they too had read the stories of Elijah. God's bread is sufficient for life, so they begin to give, just as the widow had given to the prophet. They go about giving away what they have to make it sufficient for the masses. Their success in restoring strength and life to the crowds corresponds to the success in restoring their own challenge. The bread is sufficient for the task at hand, as bread always is. Furthermore, the bread succeeds in redefining the community. At first, the disciples did not want to feed the crowds. The hungry people were the "others" who should go elsewhere to get their bread. The bread breaks even those human-constructed boundaries of otherness and builds the oneness of community. Together, the problem is solved. The version of this feeding story in the Gospel of John is even more explicit about this: The solving of the problem begins only when the disciples widen the boundaries of their community to include a boy with a little bit of food (John 6:8–9). Bread is sufficient for community, just as it is for the task and for life.

Breaking of Bread

When Jesus broke bread at the Passover meal that we commemorate as communion, it was a redefinition of the community. The Passover celebrates the formation of the Jewish community; Jesus' commemoration of that identity also celebrates the new unity of those who gather around that table. It also was a giving of responsibility to the disciples present, since they became aware of Jesus' coming departure, after which they would be charged with carrying on the task. The breaking of bread was a giving of life, as would be experienced only through Jesus' imminent death.

To celebrate communion today is to join in the long tradition of God's gift of bread. The bread partakes of the Sabbath tradition of rest and restoration. It is for the priests, but it is also for everyone. The bread allows no limits. Its marvelous sufficiency brings life, a task, and a community.

These characteristics of bread form a framework for our celebrations of this modern, yet ancient, supper of bread. Communion is a celebration of life. To emphasize communion as a memorial of Jesus' death is certainly appropriate, but it is incomplete. The bread of communion brings us life, new life, sufficient life. Likewise, communion is a task-oriented celebration. We are not just given the gift of life with which to do as we please; the life given by God's holy bread must be used in the completion of God's tasks. Thus we must use communion as a time to recall for the congregation the tasks that God has set before us. Communion may be a time of quiet reflection, but it is not a call to passivity; it is a divine command to undertake the job at hand and it is an empowering for that task. The community-building nature of bread must be part of our communion celebrations as well. Communion is a time to bridge gaps, to forge new bonds. All who partake of the elements around a common table—whether around the Lord's Table in one room or around the many across the world—become part of one family. Communion does not allow any other distinctions to be drawn; on the contrary, all other boundaries must be dismantled as we celebrate the bread of communion.

When broken, bread is divided so that it can be distributed. As the bread is passed around, it restores and heals. It brings life, it brings a task, and it brings the people into community.

4

the cup
of
judgment

Some things are just meant to go together. The words form natural pairs in our minds. For example, consider salt and pepper. This pair is so established that it's surprising to see only one on a table or to taste only one of these seasonings in food. If one asks for one at the dinner table, both are passed. Salt and pepper are a pair; our minds take the shortcut from either one to both together. We have many such pairs or groupings in our minds: window and curtain, milk and honey, hill and vale, bread and butter, rain, sleet, and snow, wine and cheese.

One such customary pair firmly set in the human mind is bread and water, the "staples of life." They are the basic food elements for humans, at least in the Western world. When food is scarce, we insist on bread and water for all, even if there is nothing else. Bread and water are the stereotypic food of prisoners and soldiers. Although other food is more desirable, bread and sustain life. In the same way, the bread of communion symbolizes the basic food needed for spiritual survival and celebrates the assurance that God provides sufficiently for that survival of the soul. Continuing this line of thought, one would expect that communion's other element would be water, not wine.

As a symbol of God's care and provision, water certainly receives favorable attention in the Old Testament. God leads the people beside still waters in Psalm 23. In the wilderness, the Israelites wash down their sufficient bread of manna with God-given water from miraculous fresh springs (Exodus 17:1–7). If water was part of communion, we could reflect solemnly on the

51

painful failures of faith condemned in Jeremiah 2:13: "For two
evil things have my people done: they have forsaken me, the
spring of living water, to dig out for themselves wells, shattered
wells that cannot contain water." Then we could celebrate the
grace and power of this sacrament with calls such as "You will
joyfully draw water from the springs of salvation" (Isaiah 12:3)
and "Everyone who thirsts, come to the waters!" (Isaiah 55:1).
What wonderful images for communion would be possible if the
second element was water!

But water is not part of communion; instead, wine is paired
with bread. The food is basic and common; the drink is valuable
and special.[1] Wine is also dangerous. We are warned by
Proverbs 20:1 that "wine is a babbler...; all who stagger because
of it have no wisdom." There are other warnings about wine:

> Do not look at wine when it is red, when it winks its eye
> in the cup—it will go straight down. In the end it bites like
> a snake and poisons like a viper. Your eyes will see
> strange objects; your heart will speak perverse things.
>   Proverbs 23:31–33

Such hardly sounds like the drink for worship! Nevertheless,
wine forms the second half of communion. In an unexpected
surprise, wine takes the place as an element of communion that
might be expected for water, despite the well-known dangers of
wine.[2]

Expected water and unexpected wine combine in the story
of the Cana wedding feast, when Jesus turns water into wine.
When faced with water, Jesus does the unexpected and gives us
miraculous wine, just as communion gives us wine instead of
the expected water. The story becomes interesting when the
spectacular party of the wedding feast has run out of wine, and
Mary, Jesus' mother, orders the host's servants to do exactly
what Jesus instructs. Jesus is not quite willing to enter into the
problem, but he relents and makes a few cryptic comments
before he disappears from the scene:

---

[1] At least, our culture grants a special value to wine. In the ancient
world, wine seems to have been the more common drink, perhaps
because of problems with the safety of the water supply. As the normal
fare for all people, wine was typically paired with bread.

[2] Of course, the Old Testament also provides many positive images
for wine, such as Psalm 104:14–15.

Six stone water jugs for the rites of Jewish purification had been set there, each containing twenty or thirty gallons. Jesus said to them, "Fill the jugs with water." They filled them to the top. He said to them, "Now, draw some out, and take it to the chief steward." So they took it. When the chief steward tasted the water that had become wine and did not know where it came from (though the servants who had drawn the water knew), the chief steward called the bridegroom and said to him, "Everyone serves the good wine first, and the the inferior wine after the guests have become drunk. But you have kept the good wine until now."

                                                    John 2:6–10

Of course, the chief steward was wrong. The best wine had not been saved for the last. The bridegroom had only an insufficient amount of wine and the party used it all up, both good and bad, much too soon. Jesus saved the situation for both the steward and the bridegroom, though they never knew what had happened. Mary was the one with insight and action; the manual laborers were the ones who saw; the disciples had belief because of this revelation of Jesus' glory. The irony of the story stands out even more clearly when one realized that the party guests, Mary and Jesus, saw the problems behind the scenes when the steward and the bridegroom were unaware of any potential for disaster. The hosts should have been finding solutions, but they did not even know what was happening. With similar irony, Jesus takes water that should be used for religious sanctification and converts it into alcohol to serve to an already-drunk crowd, and John tells the reader that this action reveals Jesus' glory to those who can see. Such things are hardly to be expected, but such is the nature of wine. Wine is dangerous and unexpected

The wine of communion always manages to confound expectations. Jesus turned the waters of ritual purity into wine for a raucous party.[3] Even today, when we expect to find religious sanctification in the wine of communion, our expectations are confounded. Instead, in communion's wine we find a

---

[3]This also symbolizes the truth of Jesus' new innovations, according to Gillian Feeley-Harnik, *The Lord's Table: Eucharist and Passover in Early Christianity* (Philadelphia: University of Pennsylvania Press, 1981), p. 60.

revelation of a God who is unexpected and quite dangerous. Such is the nature of wine.

The Cup of God's Wrath

Several Old Testament texts dealing with the cup express the dangerousness of wine. God gives many cups to the people, including the cup of God's wrath, which at some terrible times God gives. Usually, those who receive this cup are evil nations. Perhaps this is clearest in one of Jeremiah's oracles against the nations.

> For thus Yahweh, God of Israel, said to me: Take this cup of the wine of wrath from my hand and make all the nations to whom I send you drink it. When they drink, they will stagger and become insane because of the sword that I send among them.
>
> Jeremiah 25:15–16

Wine is the symbol for God's destruction, which the prophet distributes in the cup of God's wrath to those nations deserving of punishment. Here Jeremiah participates in a popular prophetic tradition of condemning other nations for their failure to perform God's tasks. Perhaps those first hearing the prophecies against the nations could feel smug and self-satisfied—after all, the prophet was condemning others, not the faithful of Israel. But Jeremiah continues:

> Then I took the cup from Yahweh's hand, and I made all the nations to whom Yahweh sent me drink it: Jerusalem and the cities of Judah, its kings and leaders, to make them a devastation and a desolation, an object of hissing and cursing, as they are today.
>
> Jeremiah 25:17–18

Jeremiah's condemnation continues with a long list of other nations, but the most important one is at the start of the list. The cup begins with Jerusalem! The people who should have been faithful are the ones who drink first from the cup of God's wrath. God forces the people of faith to drink the cup.

> If they refuse to take the cup from your hand to drink, say to them: Thus says Yahweh of hosts: You must drink! Upon the city that is called by my name, I begin to bring disaster. How can you possibly avoid punishment by yourselves?
>
> Jeremiah 25:28–29a

As is the case over and over again in the Old Testament, God does not allow resistance. The inevitable punishment that is delivered in the cup of wrath will come for all the people of faith, to all those who live in the city called by God's name, and there can be no exceptions. In a later reflection on this tradition of the cup, Jeremiah considers a common problem in Old Testament thought: do the guilty and the innocent receive punishment together, both earned and unearned? Jeremiah's frightening answer is yes.

> For thus says Yahweh: Consider those for whom there is no justice to drink the cup—must they drink it? For such are you, so innocent. But you are not innocent, so you must drink.
>
> Jeremiah 49:12

Those for whom God's cup of wrath does no good still must drink it. Such news is terrible, far beyond comprehension. It fits Jeremiah's historical situation, when the military destruction of the nation seemed inevitable and the economic and religious devastation had already begun. The people of Jeremiah's day had lost their religious sense. The wells that had held the water from their living fountain, their God, had been cracked; without water to quench the thirsts of their souls, they were forced to drink the wine of God's wrath.

The language of wine as the destruction brought by God does not end with Jeremiah; other prophets and poets share in the use of these images for their own thinking about God's action in the world. Ezekiel presents a horrific allegory of Judah's destruction. In his picture, Judah plays the younger sister of Israel. Just as Israel drank from the cup of God's wrath, so God now requires Judah to drink.

> In the path of your sister you have walked; I will give her cup into your hand. Thus says Lord Yahweh: The cup of your sister you shall drink, deep and wide; you shall be scorned and ridiculed, it contains so much. You shall be filled with drunkenness and torment. A cup of horror and desolation is the cup of your sister Samaria.
>
> Ezekiel 23:31–33

For Ezekiel, as well as for Jeremiah, the cup is a symbol of God's unavoidable wrath. God will accomplish the divine intentions, despite the preferences and wishes of persons and nations. When humans stand in the way of God, destruction is God's unstoppable tool for restoring the divine will. It is not done without sadness and divine regret about the abject horror that it entails, but the devastation wrought by God's cup of wrath occurs anyway.

The rightness of the judgment embodied in the cup of God's wrath repeats as a theme in Revelation, a book that uses much Old Testament imagery to comment on the situation of early Christians. In chapter 16 there are seven bowls filled with the wrath of God. These bowls are poured out upon the earth as God's punishment. The third angel celebrates the pouring of the bowl that turns water to blood:

> "Righteous are you, who are and were, O Holy One, because you judged these things. Because they shed the blood of saints and prophets, you have given them blood to drink. They deserve it!" And I heard the altar say, "Yes, O Lord, God Almighty, true and righteous are your judgments!"
>
> Revelation 16:5–7

This cup, filled with God's wrath instead of with soothing water, removes the water from the earth, as punishment for the sins of the world. The sins are the killing of the faithful. God provides blood for the sinners to drink; this blood pours forth from the cup of judgment. When the angels sing in celebration, even the altar in the heavenly temple breaks forth in singing, because the sinful people so well deserve God's actions. As always, it is God's justice that is at stake. Justice, not punishment, is the key characteristic of God, as the cup of wrath depicts.

In the Revelation text, the faithful ones are the victims and God's justice is involved in punishing the others. Habakkuk uses the image differently: It is Israel that has caused its neighbors to drink the cup of destruction, but now God forces Israel to drink:

> Alas for you who make your neighbors drink from the bowl of your wrath until they are drunk enough to gaze on their nakedness! You will be sated with dishonor, not glory. Drink, you yourself, and stagger! The cup in Yahweh's right hand will come around to you, and shame will cover your glory! The violence of Lebanon will overwhelm you, and the destruction of the animals will

terrify you—because of human bloodshed and violence
to the earth, to cities and all who live in them.
                                        Habakkuk 2:15–17

Habakkuk's original interpretation of the cup tradition, in
which Israel has passed the cup to others before drinking of it
itself, extends the meaning beyond that of the other passages.
The cup comes to Israel as punishment for the nation's sin of
visiting destruction on others. The violence done to others will
be done to Israel, as they deserve. God's role in bringing justice
proceeds by destroying the aggressor, Israel.

Here the point of the cup metaphor becomes apparent. The
cup of wrath is God's device for bringing the world again into the
right condition. When nations have removed justice and peace
from the face of the earth, God removes those nations. The cup
of wrath is a cup that restores justice to the world. God's
concern is the presence of justice in the world; those who would
block justice, through acts of aggression or other sins, must be
removed. Ideas of punishment based on retribution are not
appropriate descriptions of God's activity here, because the
intent of God is not to take revenge upon the sinners. God
directs action in order to stop the problem of sin and its results
at the source: by forcefully, violently removing the sinner. God
takes such activity only in extreme situations; God's cup of
destruction is a last resort after more subtle approaches have
failed. The wine God gives is dangerous, but it is salvation
because it removes a greater danger from the world.

God's actions in removing sin seem sharp and too severe to
Christians, who have been trained with stories of God's love,
mercy, and forgiveness. With the cup of wrath, God is acting in
ways that are frightening and difficult to understand. It must be
stressed that love and mercy are still at work, even in these horrible
depictions of a judgmental God. In the speech of today, God's love
is a tough love. God's love means a deep and inviolable commitment to the protection and survival of the whole human race, and
this means that there must be justice and righteousness. The world
must conform to the order that God intends for it. When the world
moves away, because of human greed or violence, God must
restore the world to its rightful place. Those who are damaging the
world by removing justice and oppressing the disadvantaged must
be stopped at any cost. The extent of the love can be measured
by the extent of the price God will pay to end injustice.

The latter part of the book of Isaiah develops the cup metaphor to its conclusion. The historical setting of this new oracle is not the same as that of Jeremiah's prophecies. Jeremiah faced the impending invasion and exile of his nation, but the prophet who preaches this new oracle in the book of Isaiah lived in the midst of the exile. The devastation of Jerusalem had already happened and the people had been deported to Babylon, where they now longed for an end to that exile. God's destruction had come and, it was hoped, its course would soon be over. This prophet begins by mourning the past devastation brought by the cup of God's wrath.

> Rouse yourself, rouse yourself! Get up, O Jerusalem, you who have drunk at the hand of Yahweh the cup of God's wrath, who have drunk to the dregs the bowl of staggering.
>
> Isaiah 51:17

God held forth this cup and offered it to the chosen people, but the cup turned out to be a cup of devastation. God's wine proved dangerous, as always. The exile was understood theologically as the people's separation from God and from the worship of God possible in the temple. The cup of God's wrath had poured forth destruction on the temple and thus had ended the possibilities for worship, but now there is a hint of hope within the deepest despair. The bowl has been completely drunk; even the dregs are now consumed. God's cup of wrath is empty.

> Therefore hear this, you are wounded, who are drunk, but not with wine. Thus says your Lord, Yahweh: your God pleads the cause for God's people. I take from your hand the cup of staggering; you shall never again drink from the bowl of my wrath.
>
> Isaiah 51:21–22

The people's time of experiencing God's destruction is over. The cup is empty and God now takes it away. A time of restoration is at hand; for this reason the prophet calls to the people: "Rouse yourself, rouse yourself! Get up, O Jerusalem!" (Isaiah 51:17). The people have drunk themselves unconscious on the wine of God's cup; now they should arise and begin again. The cup of God's wrath brought exile and suffering, but the cup has passed and the people should arise to face a new day of restoration.

> Awake, awake, clothe yourself with strength, O Zion! Put
> on your beautiful garments, O Jerusalem, the holy city!
> The uncircumcised and the unclean shall enter you
> never again! Shake yourself from the dust, rise up, O
> captive Jerusalem! Loosen the bonds from your neck, O
> captive daughter Zion!
>
> Isaiah 52:1–2

Exile ends; the passing of the cup brings a day with new
possibilities. Jerusalem is once more the holy city of God. God
is again the protector of the city, keeping out those who would
damage it. After the cup has passed back into God's hands, then
there is release and freedom from captivity.

The wine in God's cup is dangerous. It is a wine of judgment
that brings disaster and destruction to those who deserve it. It
is wine of justice that restores the intended order of the world
by putting some persons and nations back into their place, so
that others are protected. This wine restores and protects, but
for those who are not in their appointed place in the world, the
wine destroys. Some violate the order of the world by military
expansion across borders, leaving refugees to wander and
starve. Others violate God's intended world order by refusing
to worship God properly. For that reason, Israel's religious
unfaithfulness resulted in their removal from the land. In
Revelation, the theme of God's dangerous wine returns when
other nations slaughter the faithful; the murderers' violation of
God's will brings God's cup to their lips, and then the angels
sing God's justice. God's wine is dangerous for a simple reason:
God's justice is dangerous to all those who live in violation of
God's choices for life in this world. For those who live faithfully,
the wine should not be harmful. But the danger is still there in
the cup. We cannot control its power or predict its effects. In the
cup is life and death, and our choices can become known in the
drinking.

The Cup of Judgment

Some people will argue that these ancient ideas of the cup
of God's wrath are not relevant to the New Testament images
of communion's cup. Wrath, it would be said, is alien to the God
who is depicted in the New Testament as love. Justice, it would
be added, is best approached through peace, not by way of

punishment. The communion cup is a gift of God, a cup of grace and peace.

Certainly, there are many new and different ideas in the New Testament. Furthermore, the New Testament texts do not explicitly apply the cup of wrath metaphor to the practice and theology of communion. Although the New Testament's book of Revelation depicts the cup of wrath in terms very similar to those used by the Old Testament prophets, the more standard eucharistic passages in the Gospels and in the writings of Paul do not discuss the cup in these terms.

However, there are passages in the New Testament that use the language of judgment and justice to describe communion. Too often, the church ignores these texts. Certainly, they are unpleasant; these texts show a darker side to communion. Paul's lengthy discussion of communion in the first letter to the Corinthians provides such a New Testament text. Paul's comments on communion begin with 1 Corinthians 11:17, dealing with problems of factions in the Corinthians church. Then, Paul's best known communion text follows.

> For I received from the Lord what I also passed on to you, that the Lord Jesus on the night when he was betrayed took bread, and after giving thanks, he broke it and said, "This is my body that is for you. Do this in remembrance of me." Likewise, he took the cup after supper, saying, "This cup is the new covenant in my blood. Do this, as often as you drink it, in remembrance of me." For as often as you eat this bread and drink the cup, you proclaim the Lord's death until he comes.
>
> 1 Corinthians 11:23–26

This standard communion text is well known in churches today. Paul here connects the historical event of the Last Supper with the church's remembrance of it as the Lord's Supper, which Christ's followers practice in their assemblies. Often the celebration of the Lord's Supper uses these exact words. The phrase "do this in remembrance of me" has become synonymous with communion. Several of the theological interpretations here introduced and furthered by Paul have become keys to the standard theology of communion. Despite the church's high level of familiarity with and dependence upon this text, the church's worship and theology rarely continues to read the rest of the passage, which develops the possible negative consequences of the practice of communion.

> Therefore, whoever eats the bread or drinks the cup of the Lord in an undeserving manner will be liable for the body and the blood of the Lord. Test yourselves; only then eat of the bread and drink of the cup. For all who eat and drink without discerning the body, eat and drink judgment against themselves. For this reason many of you are weak and ill, and some have died. But if we judged ourselves, we would not be judged. But when we are judged by the Lord, we are disciplined, so that we may not be condemned along with the rest of the world.
>
> 1 Corinthians 11:27–32

The claims of this passage astonish most readers of the New Testament. Here, in the description of one of the most distinctive and significant Christian sacraments, one finds the shocking statement that communion can be—and actually has been—fatal. Communion, according to Paul, should not be taken lightly, but persons of faith should join in communion only after introspection, lest they "eat and drink judgment against themselves."

The cup is a powerful agent of purification. The community discovers its own true nature around the table. Those who have properly discerned the body of Christ beforehand partake of communion without risk of injury to themselves. On the other hand, Paul mentions that some have become ill or have died as a result of joining in communion without discerning the body.

What does it mean to "discern the body"? The reader can find the answer in the opening of Paul's discussion about communion. In 1 Corinthians 11:17–22, Paul condemns the factions present in the Corinthian church.[4]

> When you come together, it is not really to eat the Lord's supper. Each of you goes ahead with the eating of your own supper, and one goes hungry and another becomes drunk.
>
> 1 Corinthians 11:20–21

---

[4] See Gerd Theissen, "Social Integration and Sacramental Activity: An Analysis of 1 Cor. 11:17–34," in *The Social Setting of Pauline Christianity: Essays on Corinth* (Philadelphia: Fortress Press, 1982), pp. 145-174.

For Paul, this activity shows contempt for God's church. It may be that this refers to what Paul calls "discerning the body." To discern the body is to recognize the commonality of all persons of faith. God intends the church to be one; to discern the body is to accept God's intention and to work in that direction. Paul understands the whole community as a body—Christ's body (1 Corinthians 12:12–31). In this body, all people play vital parts. There is amazing diversity within the body, to the extent that some parts look nothing like the other parts. Still, the body is one. Within all of this diversity, unity of purpose identifies and defines the community.

The cup of communion, then, functions in two directions at once. For those who are building the church into one body, communion is a chief symbol and reality for that union. It is the proper togetherness of God's people around the table that binds them to God and to each other. For those who reject the unity of God's people, however, communion functions as a judgment that demonstrates the problem to the whole church and works to restore the unity of the church, at great cost.[5] Communion, in both bread and wine, expresses, protects, and restores the unity of the church. Those who violate this unity, which God intends, are subject to judgment.

Though the Old Testament's metaphor concerning the cup of wrath does not appear directly in the New Testament communion texts, Paul's warning in 1 Corinthians 11 strikes an amazingly similar note. In the Old Testament prophetic texts, God's cup of wine is dangerous. For those who have abrogated divine justice, the cup brings wrath and destruction, in order to

---

[5] The practical implications of this statement are immense. Communion proclaims judgment upon those who exclude others from the table. This can apply to those who fracture Christ's body by preventing women from serving at the table, as well as those who limit the table fellowship to people of a certain race, economic standing, or creed. Within this understanding, the exclusion of children from the table becomes troublesome. Of course, children have not yet reached the fullness of belief, but adults need to recognize two things: not even the church's greatest, oldest saint has attained fullness of faith, since faith keeps growing; and the exclusion of any from God's table fractures Christ's body. Children are often among the weakest parts of God's people and Christ's body, and so they are the ones who need the greatest care and the clearest statements of inclusion (1 Corinthians 12:22).

restore the order of the world as God intends. Similarly, the cup of wine that is part of communion can also be dangerous. For those who have not invited all of God's people into full participation with them in the celebration of communion, there is judgment. When the cup is passed, the danger is still present.

The Cup and the Holy of Holies

In many ways, communion's cup of judgment functions in the same way as the ancient Israelite Holy of Holies. This innermost part of the tabernacle (and later the Jerusalem temple) was God's special abode. It was a mysterious place, which only the high priest could enter once a year, on the Day of Atonement, called Yom Kippur. When King Solomon dedicated the temple, he called it a place of "thick darkness" where God would dwell (1 Kings 8:12). No light could ever reach into the Holy of Holies through the heavy curtains that shrouded it. Inside the Holy of Holies, God was safe from prying eyes and the people of Israel were safe from the possible dangers of God's presence.[6]

The instructions to Aaron, the first high priest, about Yom Kippur are lengthy and detailed (Leviticus 16). The high priest enters inside the Holy of Holies on Yom Kippur after a thorough cleansing, wearing special holy robes, and bringing with him the blood from a freshly sacrificed bull and goat. The atonement brings purification to the altar and the sanctuary, to make the next year's sacrifices effective for the people. During the time when all of this takes place, all other people must leave the area of the tabernacle or the temple, even the outer areas where people are normally allowed. Aaron has good reason to listen to these instructions very carefully; his two sons died because of their violation of the holiness of the tabernacle (Leviticus 10:1–7), and Aaron's death is at stake if he does not follow these rules exactly.

The people of ancient Israel lived with this mysterious place of great power in their midst, and so it is not surprising that many stories and popular traditions arose concerning it. There is a

---

[6] For more information about the Holy of Holies and its place within Israelite worship, see John G. Gammie, *Holiness in Israel,* Overtures to Biblical Theology (Minneapolis: Fortress Press, 1989), 9–23.

rabbinic tale of the high priests' annual entry into the Holy of Holies on Yom Kippur. On that occasion, the forgiveness of sin for all the people would have already been attained, but then the priest would have to approach God directly for his own forgiveness. The story goes that one year, God struck the priest dead while the priest was inside the Holy of Holies. The people were faced with a dilemma: Should they defile the Holy of Holies by leaving a dead body there or should they violate God's holy place by sending someone other than a high priest inside to retrieve the corpse and continue the ritual? The body was left for the Yom Kippur service of the next year when the subsequent high priest removed it. Thereafter the people insisted that the high priest tie a long rope to his foot before entering the Holy of Holies, so that if he were struck dead, others could grab the part of the rope trailing outside the curtain and pull him out. After that one horrible experience, the people were always more cautious. Their approach to the Holy of Holies carried with it a new seriousness because of their recognition of the great potential within that innermost sanctum of God.

Of course, the ancient traditions of the Holy of Holies are far from the early church's practice of communion. The cup of communion and the Holy of Holies are very different when one considers the access to God that each provides. The Holy of Holies was the place where one person, the high priest, met God once a year, on the special and fearsome day of Yom Kippur. Communion is where all Christian people meet God every time they come together. Communion offers no curtain of restriction to keep people away from the presence of God. Instead, God's presence is made available to all with great frequency. But this ease of access must not translate into a mundane experience. The high priest felt the enormous responsibility, even the dangerousness, of approaching God, and we who join in communion must do no differently.

Judgment Before the Cup

This sense of responsibility in approaching God is present in Jesus' Sermon on the Mount. In this sermon, Jesus concentrates on ethics among the faithful people, presenting a commentary on many of the Old Testament and rabbinic guidelines for action. Two of the Ten Commandments receive special attention among the many other laws mentioned, and the first of these is the commandment against murder. Jesus understands the commandment as others of his time interpreted it, but Jesus presses the case even further.

> When you bring your gift to the altar, if you remember that your brother or sister has something against you, leave your gift there before the altar and go. First be reconciled to your brother or sister, and then come and bring your gift.
>
> Matthew 5:23–24

Like the story of the Holy of Holies, Jesus regards approaching God with utmost seriousness. There are things to be done beforehand in preparation for approaching God. Jesus insists on reconciliation before one comes to the altar to bring gifts to God. Preachers have often used this text rightly to illustrate the need for reconciliation among God's people. The differences that separate us from the rest of the world must be overcome; Jesus understands this as a central and extremely urgent part of the faithful life.

But our understanding of the passage must go even further. It is essential that one reach reconciliation before one comes to the altar. Those who approach God must be purified. For Jesus, the necessary purification is reaching forgiveness and unity with others; this restores the person of faith to the order for the world that God intends. This purification must be accomplished before one approaches God. Such is also true at communion. The worshiper who approaches God at the table must be purified, or the cup itself may work that purification in dangerous ways.

Cup of Danger, Bread of Restoration

God's dangerous purification brought by the cup of communion cannot be taken lightly. Communion is not only a blessing and a gift for the church, but also a serious part of God's plan to change the world. Those who live in God's will find God present in the wine, affirming their participation in the divine intention. Those who resist God's will seek the cup only at their own risk, because the cup acts to change the world, beginning with the one who drinks. This is the power of communion—to change the world. The cup should not be avoided because of its power, but the power must be recognized and respected.

In the garden of Gethsemane, on the eve of crucifixion, Jesus faced God's cup. Jesus prayed for hours, and he repeatedly prayed to God, "If it is possible, let this cup pass away from me, but not as I wish, but as you do" (Matthew 26:39; also vs. 42, 44). Before reaching the cross, Jesus peers deeply into the cup, and only after agonizing prayer is the decision made: Jesus drinks from God's cup. Judgment and power are intermingled there, and even for Jesus, the decision to drink that cup is not made easily. But Jesus takes the cup, and the events of the next hours are sealed.

It must be emphasized that the Old Testament contains many positive images of God's cup. Not the least of these is the Twenty-Third Psalm: "you refresh my head with oil; my cup overflows" (v. 5b). God's cup brings healing and restoration for God's faithful followers, as well as security in the middle of a hostile world. Although the cup can bring restoration to God's partners, it also brings devastation to those who oppose God. Neither side can be forgotten.

Bread and wine go together in communion. Wine symbolizes the depth of God's concern for a just world by reminding the one who drinks it of the price that humanity pays with the cup of God's wrath and also of the price God paid in Jesus' outpouring of life. Justice is only purchased at great cost, but God is always willing to pay that price. We who are God's partners are also willing to share in the cost, but those who only work to make justice further away will be held responsible for their actions. God will even remove the troublemakers if such is the only way to reach justice and peace in the world. Communion wine reminds us of this high price, but the wine is not alone. The bread brings other things to mind, such as God's restoring and healing of those who hurt and the amazing sufficiency of God's bread to provide for the tasks we must do and the community that works together as God's partners. The bread speaks to us of God's support for us; wine tells us of utter seriousness of the task for which God supports us.

Bread and wine go together. Without the bread, we have a task with little hope of accomplishing it. Facing only the cup of wine, we have reason for despair, because the task of God's justice is so great. Bread's emphasis on provision and sustenance is necessary in order to come to the cup. When communion is celebrated in many churches today, the emphasis is solely on themes of bread: God cares for the people, gives to the people, saves the people. But wine must be included. Without wine, there is no challenging task to which God calls all people. Without wine, there is nothing beyond the status quo toward which to work. Without wine, there is no dangerous unexpectedness. But God is always surprising, both in grace and in commitment to save the people through justice and righteousness. To reject the danger and the surprise, as well as the challenge of partnership with God, is to reject God's intention for humanity. Bread symbolizes God's sufficiency, but the sufficient provision is for a task, for a purpose—empowerment for participation in God's activities. Wine symbolizes God's power to purify, but the purification also has a purpose—the restoration of justice throughout the world. Bread and wine go together, and both must be present in order to provide the challenge and the provisions that allow its accomplishment.

Before we partake of the cup, the questions keep coming: Are we worthy? Are we ready? Have we been part of the world's problems or part of God's solution? Partaking of the bread and sharing in God's sufficiency provides the answer, but still the question haunts us. Are we truly ready?

> But Jesus said to them, "You do not know what you are asking. Are you able to drink the cup that I drink...?" They replied, "We are able."
>
> Mark 10:38–39a

We, too, should answer that we are able to drink from the cup, but we must hope that we truly know what we are asking. Through communion, both bread and wine, we may be able to know more fully what we are asking; we may also become more able to take the cup that Jesus offers. When we accept the cup, we throw ourselves completely into God's hands. Once there, we may become able.

II

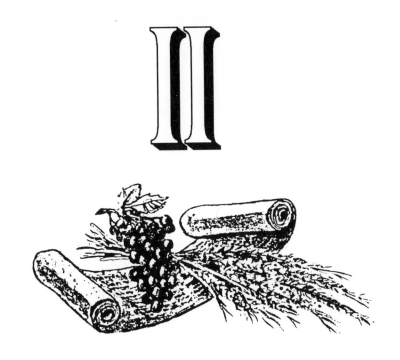

community

5

---

celebrating
the feast

It's hard to imagine a party without food. That's certainly true for the most important celebrations of the year, such as Thanksgiving and Christmas. Those parties are even known by the food that's there. Traditions may differ from family to family, but the centrality of food is usually the same. For many people, nothing brings the memories of Thanksgiving as much as a whiff of turkey roasting in the oven or the smell of cranberries. Christmas cookies baking carry their own aromas and their own memories, as does the smell of hot apple cider. If the food isn't right, it's hard to feel that you've really had a holiday. I've shared special days with people whose traditional meal was squid; I didn't enjoy that very much at all. But it works both ways—not everyone thinks of Christmas Eve as the right time for potato soup, as I do.

Not every party has a sit-down dinner with it, but almost every festive gathering has something to eat, even if it is just something to drink and a bowl of snacks. From birthday cakes and anniversary dinners to bags of potato chips during the first football games and hot dogs at the baseball parks, food and celebrations are hardly ever separated from each other. Religious celebrations are the same way, from church potlucks to the bread and wine of communion. Likewise, it's hard to imagine a solid family or a strong, vibrant church that didn't turn any shared meal into a festive occasion. Food and celebrations always go together.

The Passover Feast

Food and celebrations certainly went together during the huge Passover feasts of Jesus' time. Thousands of people would pour into Jerusalem from all over the world. They would be on a pilgrimage for the holiday. Perhaps the journey to the celebration in Jerusalem was what they did each holiday season; perhaps this would be a once-in-a-lifetime event. Jerusalem would swell with the arriving throngs; hotel space would run out long before the last round of latecomers reached the city limits. It was in the midst of such a celebration that Jesus' last supper took place.

Passover symbolized many things to one of the participating Jews, just as Christmas or Thanksgiving or Easter means many things to a modern Christian. One of those meanings was—and is—family. Passover was like a huge family reunion. Relatives from all over would gather together. New members of the extended family would be introduced to everyone else and the members lost in the previous year would be mourned in a special way. There would be the cousin that no one had seen in years and the faithful ones who were always there. Together, they would eat and celebrate the Passover, and they would also celebrate the union that they felt as family.

Friends from distant places would also gather in Jerusalem for the Passover. Perhaps they were people once known closely but now moved away; others might be people that one saw only at the big celebrations. One might even gain fresh insights on the new neighbor who still wasn't quite known. In this way, Passover was like church conventions, conferences, and assemblies in modern days, when people can see friends from all over the country. Although everyone knows we are supposed to go for the worship times, we all know we go mostly to see old friends and to make new ones. Worshiping together only serves to bring us closer together as friends, just as common meals at holidays bring families closer.

Passover was a giant family reunion and church assembly all rolled into one. The people there felt unity because of their connections. They were all part of one big family, whether related to others by genetics or by friendships. The unity was celebrated by everyone there, because everyone was glad to be part of this kind of family. Being there, all together was cause for joy and was rightly to be celebrated, in worship and in many other ways.

Passover, as well as our modern versions, created one solidified, distinct community. It set the limits of the group and made everyone inside feel together, connected, important, and wanted. The people came together from all over the world and there, through the celebration, they became one people, set apart, separate from the rest of the world. Their traditions remind them of their special nature. They belonged to God in a unique way. The celebration bonded the people together and bound them to God.

The Celebration of Communion

Communion works much the same way for the Christian church today. It is a celebration based around a mundane human experience, food, yet transcending those humble beginnings in order to symbolize the whole nature of the church. Communion celebrates a shared past, a common community in the present, and a hope for the future.

Communion memorializes a shared past. Communion's most distinctive words are "in remembrance of me," and as a celebration it focuses on the past events of Jesus' life and death. Because it focuses on Jesus' death, communion is often experienced as a solemn event, but there is certainly more at work. Communion should also commemorate all of Jesus' life and teaching, including the remarkable announcements about a coming new day when God's way of life will be followed by all peoples. It should be a moment within the church's worship that celebrates everything about Jesus, including the morality that Jesus presents as the way to life as part of God's world. Communion should be more than a solemn observance; it is not inappropriate to have partaken of the joyous past of Jesus and of the church!

Communion also celebrates a community in the present. The church is a community with varied roots and a diverse present, but it is a community that belongs together. The communion table unites all Christians, regardless of the ways in which the world would separate them.

One of my pastors recently told the following story about dogs and cats as part of a communion meditation. Many years ago when he was a child, Jim's neighbor had been riding a bicycle when he noticed a cat on the road, crushed by a passing car. He stopped to see if he could help, but the cat was dead.

Right before he got back onto the bike, he heard a faint mewing. He was confused—the cat couldn't possibly be alive! Off to the side of the road were four small kittens, no more than a few hours old. He put them in his shirt pockets and went straight home.

His family tried to feed the kittens bowls of milk, but they were too young. They tried feeding them from eyedroppers, but they were even too young for that. The family was almost out of hope for the kittens when a strange idea crossed their minds. The family's dog had just given birth to pups and was still nursing them. Tenuously, they introduced the dog to the kittens. The proverbial animosity between dogs and cats was on the top of their minds—would this mother dog allow these kittens to nurse? They took to each other right away, and the two litters became one as they nursed together. When they all grew up, those dogs and cats were never enemies; they were one family.[1] Such is the nature of communion; it brings all people together at one common table, bridging all walls of hostility. Because of this ability to find the common in the midst of difference, communion affirms diversity and denies uniformity. It is a celebration of community.

Communion anticipates a common hope for the future. The story of Jesus' ministry provides hope for a world that lives in God's love. It gives a hope that the world can be saved and will be saved through God's actions among people. The world, God affirms through Jesus, is worth saving and is worth all of God's effort to bring this salvation to fruition. In the present, communion reminds us of the tasks of morality and faithfulness that are part of God's work in the world, including God's work through Jesus. Because the community of faith shares responsibility for the world, there are tasks that we can do now, and God gives us the hope that these tasks are not in vain. The present of communion leads inexorably to the future of hope, and the hope in the future calls us forward to do our work in God's name in the present. Salvation will arrive, and our task is to be working on God's behalf in preparation for the coming salvation.

The hope for the future can be seen clearly in the Old Testament's visions about a feast to be shared at some future time. Then the community will be present and unified and the common past will be remembered and put into practice. God's

---

[1] My thanks to Jim Robinson, associate pastor of Harvard Avenue Christian Church (Disciples of Christ), Tulsa, Oklahoma, for his permission to use this story, which he told on September 16, 1990.

someday feast will be a marvelous celebration, a gigantic party, focusing on God's own presence with the people who are called together into community. Past, present, and future all come together in the someday feast, as they do in every communion service.

The Someday Feast

Communion is a celebration, like the ancient feasts and festivals of the faith. The Old and New Testaments also talk about feasts in the future. These will be marvelous feasts that bring the whole people of God together in celebration. These feasts not only give thanks for God's goodness, but also recognize the coming of a new way of life among those who follow God. The peple excitedly anticipate these future feasts. As they talk about how things will be when that someday feast comes, they dream about the peace and harmony that is possible among God's people.

Within the Old Testament, a shining example of this expectation of a someday feast can be found in Zechariah 7—8. A delegation comes to the prophet Zechariah from the outlying city of Bethel. They come with a question about the proper form of worship to observe.

> "Should I mourn and abstain in the fifth month, as I have done for many years?"
>
> Zechariah 7:3

The seventh day of the fifth month had been a time of fasting for the past seventy years, commemorating the destruction of Jerusalem and its temple when the Babylonians conquered Judah and took the people into exile.[2] Now, some of the Jewish people have returned and have begun to live again in the land of their grandparents. Since their time of separation from the land was over, was there still a need to commemorate the past destruction? Such was the question facing the prophet Zechariah, whose answer comes at the end of the next chapter.

> The word of Yahweh of hosts belonged to me, saying,
> "Thus says Yahweh of hosts: The fast of the fourth

---

[2] Carol L. Meyers and Eric M. Meyers, *Haggai, Zechariah 1—8*, Anchor Bible 25B (Garden City, New York: Doubleday, 1987), pp. 379–394, 433–434.

month, and the fast of the fifth, and the fast of the
seventh, and the fast of the tenth should be for the house
of Judah joy and gladness, good festivals."

Zechariah 8:18–19a

Zechariah's answer might well have shocked the people.
The proper respect for the past, as expressed in the solemn fasts
on four different days throughout the year, was no longer
important, according to this prophet. The people were to fast no
more in memory of the detroyed temple or for the bygone,
glorious days of Israel. Instead, the people were to feast and
celebrate joyously. Their glad-hearted celebration was to become infectious and spread to all four of the days of fasting.
Everything was to be affected by the newfound joy. God spread
the table of feasting and spread it so large that it covered the
whole year. Past pain was displaced and replaced by the new
celebration. Zechariah's response continues to demonstrate
how wide God's table of celebration is:

"Thus says Yahweh of hosts: Then peoples shall come,
who dwell in numerous cities. The inhabitants of one city
shall go to another, saying, 'Come, let us go to entreat
the favor of Yahweh, and to seek Yahweh of hosts; I
myself am going.' Numerous peoples and strong nations
shall come to seek Yahweh of hosts in Jerusalem, and to
entreat the favor of Yahweh. Thus says Yahweh of hosts: In
those days ten men from nations of every language shall
grasp a Jew by the hem and say, 'Let us go with you, for we
have heard that God is with you.'"

Zechariah 8:20–23

How infectious is the celebration! Not only are all the Jews
of Jerusalem involved throughout the year, but the party grows
beyond the borders. People from different cities come to the
celebration. Those who are coming to the celebration are so
overflowing with excitement that they evangelize along the way.
They seek out others to spread the exhilaration. The anticipation for the party expands across all boundaries of city or nation.
Politics and ethnicity, race and economic boundaries are all
suddenly, magnificently irrelevant, because the people of the
whole world are hearing about God and are excited about what
they hear. Ten persons from all over the world grab hold of one
of God's followers, asking for directions along the way to God's

own celebration. The sudden explosion of interest in God's way of life brings new persons of faith who outnumber and even overrun the old-time faithful. Reserved seats and old traditions are set aside in the onrush of new celebrants.

What is it that creates all of this excitement? The people of the world have caught a glimpse of what life can be like when God's people love truth and peace (Zechariah 8:19). It is truly cause for celebration! In the verses between the delegation's question about the old fasts (Zechariah 7:3) and the prophet's announcement of the new feasts (Zechariah 8:19) are the reasons for the excitement. Zechariah presents a vision of what can be, if people follow God's direction in life. The vision begins by reminding the people of what God has always said:

> "Render true judgments,
> perform kindness and compassion to each other.
> Do not oppress the widow,
> > the orphan,
> > the alien,
> > the poor;
> and do not devise evil in your hearts against each other."
> > Zechariah 7:9–10

These simple instructions form a summary of the guidelines for life that God gave in the Torah and throughout the nation's history. Then the remarkable results are detailed:

> Thus says Yahweh: I will return to Zion, and will dwell in the midst of Jerusalem. Jerusalem will be called the faithful city, and the mountain of Yahweh of hosts shall be called the holy mountain.
> > Zechariah 8:3

If the people will listen to God's instructions and will obey these basic rules for life, then God will live in the midst of the people. The Creator of the universe will take up residence in the center of the people's city. The whole city will gain the reputation earned by their faith. That reputation will generate the excitement among the peoples of the nations that will bring them streaming to Jerusalem.

From this beginning, the vision grows more specific. Zechariah has stated that God will be present among the people and that the close relationship between God and people will be known throughout the world. We have also seen the results of that knowledge as others are excited about and attracted to God's celebration in the faithful city, Jerusalem. Now, the prophet's vision turns toward the specifics of life in the city perched on God's holy mountain.

> Thus says Yahweh of hosts: Old men and old women shall again sit in the streets of Jerusalem, each with staff in hand because of their great age. And the streets of the city shall be filled with boys and girls playing in its streets. Thus says Yahweh of hosts: Even though it seems impossible to the remnant of this people in these days, should it also seem impossible to me, says Yahweh of hosts?
>
> Zechariah 8:4–6

This vision is remarkable in the simplicity of its image and the distance between this vision and modern American reality. In Zechariah's vision, the city's elderly are safe on the streets, where they can sit together and enjoy one another's company. Each one holds a staff, helping them to navigate safely and working to provide their basic needs of mobility. The staffs in their hands are also symbols of honor and respect, demonstrating their notable accomplishment of advanced age. These are the survivors who have seen hard times, and the community values their collective wisdom and tradition.

Along with the elderly who sit in the streets with respect are the children who play in Jerusalem's boulevards. They too are safe there, even though they are unsupervised. All the children play together with joy, without arguing or fighting, but with the unity of God's people. Divisions of family, class, or wealth are not part of this picture; there is only harmony.

Zechariah's vision is in sharp contrast to the contemporary scene. In modern America, the elderly and children alike are among the most unprotected members of the society. They cannot defend themselves and so they are the most common victims of all sorts of violence and abuse. Hunger and crime run rampant among their ranks, as most of society refuses to offer the kind of help needed. When faced with the deep problems of the youngest and the oldest, our society would prefer to listen to special interests with more lobbying power. The oppression of the weak is so deeply ingrained that it seems unstoppable.

The people in Zechariah's day agreed, though for different reasons. They had seen the military destruction of Jerusalem by the Babylonians and they still lived in a time of fear. Other military threats loomed large on the horizon; the destruction might return at any moment. In the meantime, the people were poor, and work was needed from everyone. Even the elderly and the children were required to work in the fields and in other occupations in order to keep food on the families' tables. To imagine a day when life could be anything else would have been a daring dream. The people would have said that such peace and prosperity was impossible. God heard the people's complaint and asked, "Do you think that it also seems impossible for me?" (Zechariah 8:6). God knew full well the difficulties and hardships of the people; God in no way wished to negate the people's own painful experience. Nevertheless, God sends a vision of a day when things will be different, and the vision carries a challenge: It could be like this, if you follow.

Zechariah has presented a vision of peace and harmony for the young and the old alike. In the vision, no one is threatened because of their lack of physical power. Instead, all persons have the right to enjoy all the times of their lives in appropriate ways. Together the young and old celebrate God's peace in the streets of the city. God throws a huge feast on this miraculous someday, and all the people join in, regardless of age or potential for productivity. As impossible as this vision seems, Zechariah continues to explain what he sees, and that includes even more universal visions of safety and restoration.

> Thus says Yahweh of hosts: I am saving my people from the east and from the west; I will gather them and they shall live in Jerusalem. They shall be my people and I will be their God, in faithfulness and in righteousness.
> Zechariah 8:7–8

Just as the age and power boundaries will be dismantled in God's new day, there will be a dramatic end to divisions of race and geography. In Zechariah's time as in our own, bringing east and west together means overcoming separations of economics and politics as well as ethnicity and nationality. People of religion might well include the categories of denomination and religious perspective along with the disagreements that become suddenly and permanently irrelevant. Our society today has managed much more division than Zechariah's time; perhaps we would need to expand the list to proclaim the end of many other separations, such as those based on economic status and gender.

All such divisions have no place at God's great someday feast. People will choose only one appellation; they will call themselves "God's people." No other name or identity will make any sense at all. Once the people have come together at God's feast, there no longer will be any desire to be separate and distinct again.

The last words demonstrate the basis for the new community of God's people. God will serve as God of all people. Although some were God's first chosen, now those boundaries are also removed. God will be everyone's God, if they will be God's people. All of this is part of God's faithfulness and righteousness (Zechariah 8:8). Because God is faithful and loyal, there will be the best possible situation of the people. God's care and provision are tantamount at God's great someday feast. God is also righteous, which guarantees protection for all persons. There can be no exploitation and no advantage to any in this vision. God demands righteousness for all people who are present at this universal celebration.

After these visions, the prophet again reminds the people of the divinely ordained guidelines for life. These straightforward instructions are the key to the visions that have just been beautifully presented. If the people will do these simple things, then the visions can come true.

> These are the things that you should do:
> Speak the truth to each other,
> render in your gates truth and judgments that make peace,
> do not devise evil in your hearts against each other,
> and love no false oath.
>
> Zechariah 8:16–17a

The instructions are simple. At the great feast, not only do the people see the beauty that can be present in human communities, but they are given God's own advice about how to make this happen. Honesty, justice, peace, good intentions, and truth are straightforward paths to the celebration. These actions will bring about God's feast. It is a plan with divinely guaranteed success, if only people will follow.

Communion today can be the same kind of celebration. Our Lord's Supper has the potential for reminding us of God's promise of a someday feast. This requires a vision of a world where God lives in our midst, where all persons in our society are safe and protected, and where all persons and nations from all over the world, regardless of their category or preferences, are called to partake of the one feast. When communion expresses this vision, it will be this kind of magnificent celebration.

But the service of communion must not stop with the expression of shared vision. It must also remind the people of God's call to the life of justice that can make this vision come true. The church of today cannot afford to stop repeating the ancient call to the faithful, moral life: speak the truth, render true justice, make peace, devise good plans, refuse falsehood. Zechariah begins and ends the prophetic vision about the possible future of God's people with statements about how people should live; the church must do the same. These are not rigid moral codes; they are simple guides for bringing this vision to our world.

If we truly communicate this vision and if we begin to enact the simple means for making it into reality, the excitement will spread almost by itself. No one could possibly stop it, even if one tried. The excitement that begins within the people of faith soon spreads throughout the rest of the area, and then it goes even further until it becomes an international yearning to be with God. When the world sees this kind of vision, a vision of magnificent celebration in just peace and righteous harmony, the enthusiasm becomes contagious, infecting the whole world.

But it is easy to be cynical, even in the midst of such a vision. In Zechariah's time, there were those who complained, "All of this is impossible. It just won't work. We have enough to do just keeping things going as they are. We have to set realistic goals. Anything this big is simply impossible." God responded to this, "Just because you think it's impossible, do you really think it's impossible for me?" God has been dreaming this impossibly simple dream long before us, long before Zechariah. Bringing it into reality is something that God has always claimed to be able to do. But first God's people must recognize their place: rendering true justice, demonstrating mercy to each other, protecting the disadvantaged, devising good plans, loving truth and peace. Zechariah brings together God's vision, full of possibilities, with the impossibly simple guides for God's people to bring it into reality. The promise is that the vision will be contagious, if God's people only do their part.

Celebrating the Removal of Death

Zechariah is not the only prophet to proclaim a vision of a magnificent someday feast when God's people live just, true lives and God is in their midst. Isaiah's version of the vision gives another expression of the glory that is waiting for God's people on that someday when the feast comes around. Isaiah depicts a celebration centered around a sensational banquet, which is offered to those who have waited for God's salvation.

> On this mountain, Yahweh of hosts will make for all peoples a feast of rich food, a feast of aged wines, of delicacies filled with richness, of aged wines strained clear. On this mountain, God will destroy the shroud that is cast over all peoples, the sheet that is spread over all nations. God will utterly destroy death. Then Lord Yahweh will wipe tears from all faces; the reproach of God's people will turn away from the whole earth, for Yahweh has spoken. It will be said on that day, "This is our God; we hoped for God and God saved us. This is Yahweh; we hoped for Yahweh—let us be glad and rejoice in God's salvation.
>
> Isaiah 25:6–9

This vision by Isaiah expresses many of the same themes as Zechariah's vision. There is good food and plenty of it; there are the festive wines for celebration. Repeatedly, the vision emphasizes that this is for all peoples, not just for a few. In both visions, it is God who saves and the people who participate in bringing this salvation into reality, but there are also differences at this point. Zechariah emphasizes the moral activity that people undertake in order to work with God in bringing the world to salvation. Isaiah, on the other hand, stresses God's work for which the people wait. It is God and God alone who saves.

The similarities between these two visions' view of God's relationship with the people, however, also deserve attention. Isaiah discusses the removal of death, which is clearly impossible for humans. Instead, the people are right to wait until God brings the salvation to them in that wonderful someday feast. Zechariah also realizes the impossibility of human action reaching the final salvation; in his vision God hears the people's claims that the work is impossible. Zechariah, however, stresses the things that people can do to move the vision closer.

In Isaiah's vision, the people wait for God. Waiting, though, cannot be considered a passive activity. It is an act of faith. Waiting can only be done when one knows where to wait and for whom to wait. It is not a waste of time; it is making sure that one is in the right place when the right time comes. Waiting is also a strong social statement of critique. Those who wait for God to bring something better are expressing their displeasure in the current situation. They are refusing to accept the status quo; they are rejecting the statements that everything is all right. Those who wait know the problems and know that God has the solutions.

To some extent, however, the vision is the solution. When the people know through their prophets the direction in which God is working, then they too can do things to move in that same direction. For Isaiah, this means being on the right mountain when God's someday feast comes. For Zechariah, God's chosen direction for the people involves moral activity that excites and enthralls the nations. The decisive actions belong to God, but for both Isaiah and Zechariah, the delivery of a vision is one of those decisive acts of God.

In Isaiah's day, things were worse for the people. Their oppression was greater and their opportunities for action were fewer. Zechariah's time provided more reasons for optimism and more chances for action. Not surprisingly then, the exact messages were different, but the overall vision remained the same. God is bringing a someday feast; when it comes there will be peace and justice, and even death will be removed. In the meantime, there are things that can be done. Peace and justice can be performed and the nations will be excited to see it. If nothing else on earth is possible, then the people should wait in the right place for that someday feast, rejecting the other visions that the world offers.

When the early church was in a situation like Isaiah's, a time of persecution and troubles, the book of Revelation was written. John's vision of a someday feast includes a new city, a new Jerusalem, to usher in the feast of newness. When the city arrives, then a voice from the throne of God sings forth, using the words of Isaiah's and Zechariah's visions:

> See, God's tent is among humans. God will dwell with them as their God; they will be God's peoples, and God will be with them and will wipe each tear from their eyes. Death will be no more; grieving and crying and affliction will be no more, for the first things have passed away.
> Revelation 21:3–4

In that new city, the banquet table is spread wide and all the nations are invited to enter the city and join the banquet. Together, the hosts invite the world to the someday feast:

The Spirit and the bride say, "Come."
And let everyone who hears say, "Come."
And let everyone who is thirsty come.
Let anyone who wishes take the water of life as a gift.
                                        Revelation 22:17

Just as in Zechariah's vision, the table is open to the world. Everyone is invited. In this vision in Revelation, however, the image goes even further. All of those who accept the invitation are asked to shout forth the invitation to others. God's faithful cannot afford to wait for the other nations to notice the special things going on in our midst; we must announce it to them. The invitation goes far and wide, and the table opens out to the whole world. Death and fear, mourning and crying and pain, have all been vanquished and removed. Let everyone come to the feast!

The World Called to Communion

The whole world, then, is the community that is called to communion. God's wide table can have no limits among the people of faith. Communion thus rejects all the world's divisiveness. In the visions of Zechariah, Isaiah, and John, geographic and political boundaries are rejected in favor of a new identity as God's people, who live in God's city. Similarly, communion as practiced in contemporary churches emphasizes one table, hosted by one Lord. All other identities and loyalties are displaced by the identity of the communion table.

Communion creates a union because it replaces division with a singular identity. Of course, diversity exists within the union; individuality is never lost around God's table. By presenting a common vision for all to share, the table gives birth to unity of purpose among all God's people. The vision attracts all God's people equally and provides the common ground for all to work together toward accomplishing this goal. Unity of task accompanies the unity of purpose. The table of communion unites God's people.

Although almost all Christians acknowledge the importance of communion, few of the church's special emphases focus on this central, shared aspect of our life of faith. Communion rarely receives the significance it deserves as a regular and frequent part of the church's worship. One of the few times during the church year when Christians do affirm the centrality of communion is during the first Sunday in October, World Communion Sunday. This day is best observed as a lively celebration of the church's unity around the table. It commemorates the church's single focus of vision and the magnificent vitality of the common task. The church's unity is experienced as a centering around a common task and as a time of joy, a season of gladness. Communion is a celebration with the whole people of God, who are united in a common task of bringing God's vision into reality. Let the party begin!

6

---

the economics
of
communion

Amazingly few times do the Gospels depict Jesus eating.
Food is such a common part of everyday life. Jesus must have
had hundreds, or thousands, of meals with the disciples during
the period of his ministry. Therefore, when one of those meals
is recorded right before the institution of the Lord's Supper, it
becomes all the more noticeable.

> When Jesus was at Bethany in the house of Simon the
> leper, a woman came to him with an alabaster jar of very
> expensive ointment. She poured it on his head as he sat
> at the table. When the disciples saw it, they were angry
> and said, "Why this waste? This ointment could have
> been sold for a large sum, and the money given to the
> poor." Jesus, knowing this, said to them, "Why do you
> cause trouble for this woman? She has performed a
> good service for me. For you always have the poor with
> you, but you will not always have me."
>
> Matthew 26:6–11

This strange little story, centered around a table during
mealtime, has been interpreted in countless ways over the
years. The woman clearly did the right thing for the time. She
anointed Jesus for burial, because Jesus' burial was near,
though the disciples had not admitted that to themselves. She
did what Jesus' closest followers could not do because they had
not yet faced the realities that were at hand in Jesus' life. For
this, she is praised, and the story notes that "wherever this good

news is preached in all the world, what she has done will be told in remembrance of her" (Matthew 26:13).

The story is clear that the woman is to be praised for her actions. She is a generous woman. She is willing to spend what she has, refusing to hoard it. She has done the right thing in her situation. The difficulty arises when we ask what we should do in response to this story. This woman has not given her money to the poor, but to Jesus in preparation for burial. Should we give our money to the poor or should we do the same as the woman and find some other use for our money? This is a difficult question.

It seems that Jesus has given some directions in answer of this question. Ointment is for burial, and so using her money for ointment is appropriate while Jesus is not yet buried. Once the death and resurrection come, burial preparations are no longer needed, and so the money can be used in other ways. In other words, we always have the poor with us, but Jesus was only here on earth with physical needs for a while. Now, the money should go to the poor.

Note also where this conversation occurs. Jesus has dined with a variety of characters in the Gospels. In this story in Matthew, he is at the home of a leper! When Luke tells this story, Jesus is at the home of a Pharisee, where all is proper, but the woman is repeatedly called a sinner.[1] Theologically, these stories keep reaffirming that all persons are called to Christ's table and to full participation in the life of Christ's followers, even today. The state of one's health, one's social standing in the community, even one's sinfulness do not stop anyone from joining Jesus around the table.

In the middle of this inclusive table fellowship, Jesus states that we will always have the poor with us. Economics and the table go together. Jesus' image of the table is inclusive economically as well as in other ways. The poor should now be the focus of our inclusivity around the table.[2]

Food and money go together. The cost of eating is one of the basic economic needs within any society. The most familiar

---

[1] Luke 7:36–50. Luke prefaces the story with the comment that Jesus has been accused of eating with tax collectors and sinners.

[2] On this issue, see Tissa Balasuriya, *The Eucharist and Human Liberation* (Maryknoll, New York: Orbis Books, 1979), especially pages 48-63.

images for money are food-related, such as "bringing home the bacon" and "earning the bread." The word "salary" comes from the Latin word for salt. Romans were often paid in salt, which was one of the few ancient ways to preserve meat. From that has come expressions such as "worth one's salt" and "working in the salt mines." Thus, not surprisingly, economics and Jesus' table are also connected.

Economics and Hospitality

The church today is rightly concerned with economics. A variety of resolutions have been prepared and passed by many denominations, supporting all sorts of economic measures, from proper compensation and health care for pastors to boycotts of certain foods in response to unjust business practices by corporations. Divestment of stock of corporations invested in South Africa has been an important economic means of showing displeasure with the evil of apartheid. The feeding of the hungry throughout the world has been a goal and an involvement for many churches, even though some of the funding mechanisms have become controversial when they feed the "wrong kind of people," such as those living under opposing political systems. The church has increasingly focused on a wide range of economic concerns.

At the same time, parts of the church have felt alienated from this emphasis on economics at the denominational level. Such actions are typically perceived as being someone else's business; some even feel that churches are not the proper avenue for such social and economic involvement. Those things belong to some other group; the church should be in the business of worshiping God, some say. It seems that such detractors have a point, though not necessarily the one that is immediately apparent.

The church has developed an almost schizophrenic nature when it comes to economics. Too often, economics have been relegated to the national levels of the church and the local churches have not been integrated into the political processes by which these things happen. But a more important division is apparent. Too often, economics is not part of worship. That is, worship never mentions the economic concerns that are legitimately part of the wider church's response to God's grace. True worship must be a response to God that includes and integrates all the other responses that we make. A sense of community with other believers is an important part of the Christian life, and it should be a sense that is cultivated and expressed in worship. The inclusion of all persons into Christ's church is an important element of our faith; this should happen in worship as well as in every other aspect of church life. This list could continue throughout all the church's beliefs and convictions. Every other element of our faith needs to be present in worship, and our convictions about economic justice are no different.

Furthermore, since communion is such an integral part of worship, there should be ways to talk about economics when we talk about the table of Jesus. One way to achieve this goal is to talk about hospitality, which is a general term for the many ways in which the Bible urges us to share what we have with others in order to demonstrate our acceptance of them in faith. Hospitality is a form of caretaking, when those who possess the goods of the world share with those who are disadvantaged to some extent. Hospitality, in its biblical usage, is a way of life, not just an occasional deed. Hospitality is also intimately connected to faith. It is not an option for social justice that some persons of faith choose as an addition to the rest of the beliefs; hospitality is an essential part of biblical faith and is commanded by God.

Hospitality appears clearly in the Old Testament's laws concerning foreigners and resident aliens. God's instructions to the Israelites forbade the exploitation of these marginal persons, just as it protected the rights and needs of the poor. This preference for the poor[3] manifests itself in God's command to provide food for the needy.

> When you harvest the bounty of your land, do not continue harvesting to the edges of your field, and do not gather the gleanings of your harvest. Do not strip bare

---

[3] "God's preferential option for the poor" has been presented in many recent books on liberation theology. The legal codes of the Old Testament usually develop the perspective that God shows no preferences to any category of humanity, whether poor or not. However, these same legal texts command that persons show the proper attitude of helpfulness toward those who most need it, such as the poor. Thus, humans should give preferential treatment to the poor. God's commands to humans to demonstrate this preference may well be regarded as a divine preference for the poor.

your vineyard, and do not gather the fallen grapes of your vineyard. Leave them for the poor and the alien: I am Yahweh your God.

Leviticus 19:9–10[4]

Our society concentrates on efficiency and productivity. We want to maximize the gain on our investments and to reap our harvests to their full potential. The biblical imperative, however, is quite the opposite. Some of the fields should be left unharvested. The farmer should grow a field full of food but should not reap all of it; instead, some should be left untouched, so that others can come and take the scraps for their own food. The poor must be allowed an opportunity for life. This also means that the wealthy are not permitted to live their own life to its fullest economic potential, because they must leave some for others.

Our society labels this as waste. To leave part of the potential untapped in order that others can gain from the labor that workers have given to their work is wasteful in the modern view. Ancient societies, such as those of the Bible, tend to see things quite differently. Wealth could only be accomplished at the expense of others; those who had wealth possessed it only because of what others did not have. Thus, the wealthy had an obligation to share. Wealth, in the religious view, existed only to allow giving from some to others. Therefore, wealth must be shared with those who do not have wealth. All persons must be given ample opportunity to survive and to eat. Wealthy persons then have ample opportunities to share their bounties and their abundances.

If there are any needy among you, a member of your community in any of your towns within the land that Yahweh your God gives you, do not be hard-hearted or tight-fisted toward your needy neighbor. Instead, open your hand, willingly lending enough to meet the need, whatever it may be....Give freely and be ungrudging when you do so, because on this account Yahweh your God will bless you in all your work and in all the deeds of your hands. Because needs will never cease upon the earth, I therefore command you, "Open

---

[4] This is repeated, almost word for word, in Leviticus 23:22.

> your hand to each other, to the poor and needy neighbor
> in your land."
>
> Deuteronomy 15: 7–8, 10–11

This text issues a call to the wealthy landowners who manage the responsibility of sharing their goods. God calls them beyond mere economic perceptions of the problems. The transfer of funds and goods is not God's goal for humanity; compassion and caregiving are part of that goal. Giving should be generous and free-spirited, not limited by concepts of legality or obligation. Instead, the laws about how much to leave in the fields for the needy are only a starting point. One must give at least as much as the law requires, but one should give generously beyond that.[5]

The Old Testament code here states the principle: There will always be the poor on earth (Deuteronomy 15:11). This quote forms Jesus' response in the story told at the start of this chapter (Matthew 26:11). Jesus' attitude toward the poor can be derived from the rest of the verse that he begins to quote: "Open your hand to the poor and needy." This attitude can be seen as a one-to-one approach to the human problem of poverty: When an individual person is in need, that individual should receive help. Other approaches are also part of God's plans for dealing with the poor, however, including establishing structures to support those who are permanently in need.

> From the harvest of every third year, bring out the full tithe of your produce for that year, and store it within your towns. Let the Levites come, because they have no allotment or inheritance with you, and also the resident aliens, the orphans, and the widows in your towns. Let them eat their fill so that Yahweh your God may bless you in all the work of your hands that you do.
>
> Deuteronomy 14:28–29

Levites, as this passage explains, have no inheritance within Israel. They were chosen to be the priestly group within the nation, and thus they never had the opportunity to engage in

---

[5] This is, in my opinion, one of the points of the book of Ruth. Boaz is legally responsible to care for Ruth and Naomi in certain limited ways; the question is whether he will find it within himself to transcend the law and provide even more, as well as whether he will give generously and freely, not reluctantly.

economic activities that produce profit and benefit. Instead, they are permanently in need, because they cannot meet their own financial needs. For this reason, the society as a whole must develop a structure—a 10 percent tax on produce in every third year—that will meet the needs of these people who are part of the nation and part of God's chosen people. Others who share the same problem as the Levites have share in this income from the third-year tithe. Orphans and widows share the disadvantage of inability to produce income sufficient for their needs in the ancient society that allowed economic productivity primarily for adult males. Because the structure of society limits these persons' abilities to provide for themselves, God commands the society to provide equitably for them. Resident aliens represent another underprivileged category. Their ethnicity limited their economic possibilities; thus, the society must compensate the inequities by finding other ways to care for them. Together, these four groups represent many different forms of social oppression: gender, age, family connection, race, ethnicity, and occupation. In God's view, society must redress all of these limitations and provide equitably for all.

The sharing of one's goods with others is the only way to enjoy God's blessings. This is not a knee-jerk, quid pro quo reaction of God who only gives to those who give back. Instead, God extends partnership. God's blessings bring prosperity, the goal is not the increase of one person's accumulation of wealth. God's prosperity allows God's other children to receive the bounty through paths of grace. God's blessings pass through open hands and so flow to the needy.

Throughout the many other laws regarding these foreigners, one general principle overrules all other considerations.

> When an alien resides with you in your land, you should not be oppressive. The alien who resides with you shall be to you as the citizen among you; you shall love the alien as yourself, because you were aliens in the land of Egypt: I am Yahweh your God.
>
> Leviticus 19:33–34

This statement from God develops the care for the disadvantaged further than the prior legal indications. The earlier instructions provided ways to bring preference to the poor after they had already been hurt by a society that limited their participation in life. A new principle enters here. The people should extend to aliens the same treatment as citizens. In other words, identical legal protection and social opportunities must exist for all, regardless of social class.

This is an amazing proposition. The other parts of the Old Testament legal code give preference to the poor after they have already been disadvantaged, but this indicates the need to prevent such economic violence before it occurs. The preference for the poor becomes an active prevention, not a stopgap bandage after the injury. The differences between persons, such as race and ethnicity, must no longer be divisions that separate economic opportunities and possibilities for life. By extending the thought, the same protection should be extended across the lines of gender, age, and occupation. These differences must not develop into divisions that limit life for some in order to benefit others. Leviticus 19:33–34 concludes with a reason for this divine insistence on equal protection within society's structures. The reason is the very nature of God, which calls for compassionate equitability for all persons within the society.

The reason for this strong tendency in ancient Israelite law is that the Israelites began as slaves in Egypt. This thought finds expression in a clear-cut statement from God.

> Do not disadvantage a resident alien; you yourselves know the heart of an alien, because you were aliens in the land of Egypt.
>
>   Exodus 23:9

The basis for right action is, as always, compassion. Experience of the hurts and sufferings of the poor and disadvantaged produces a knowledge of their plight, and this knowledge must result in the refusal to create or to allow oppression. When God invites the people as partners in the divine protection of all people, this compassion leads to equality. Such is the role of hospitality. It reaches all people because of God's desire to reach all people. Hospitality rights all wrongs, both those of the past that must be redressed and those of the future that God wishes us to prevent. Only then is true communion possible, as all join equally around God's one table, in partnership with God.

Prophetic Hospitality

The Old Testament's legal texts treat hospitality as an issue of social justice. Because there are needs in the world, the people of God must meet those needs. As legal texts always do, these present an impersonal view of the problem. Categories of persons receive attention, but one never sees the victims face to face. The prophetic texts of the Old Testament show a different side to hospitality in God's name.

The Elijah and Elisha stories portray strongly God's interest in hospitality. Over and over again, these early prophets meet persons in tragic situations and they bring God's healing to these persons.[6] Compassion combines with miracles to express the largess of God's concern with hospitality. In this story about Elisha, one of the prophet's disciples has died, leaving the disciple's widow in dire financial straits. She approaches Elisha, who responds with compassion.

> Now the wife of one of the company of prophets cried to Elisha, "Your servant my husband is dead. You know that your servant revered Yahweh, but a creditor has come to take my two children as slaves." Elisha said to her, "What shall I do for you? Tell me, what do you have in the house?" She answered, "Your servant has nothing in all the house, except a jar of oil." Elisha said, "Go outside, borrow vessels from all your neighbors. Make sure that they are empty vessels, without anything in them. Then go in, and shut the door behind you and your children, and pour into all these vessels. Set them aside when they are full." So she left him and shut the door behind her and her children. They kept bringing vessels to her, and she kept pouring. When the vessels were full, she said to her son, "Bring me another vessel." But he said to her, "There are no more." Then the oil stopped. She came and told the man of God, and he said, "Go sell the oil and repay your debts, and you and your children can live on the rest."
>
> 2 Kings 4:1–7

This widow borrows empty jugs from her neighbors and then finds them miraculously full of cooking oil, a valuable commodity that she could sell to pay her debts. God's miraculous

---

[6] Elijah and Elisha prophesy in the northern parts of Israel during the ninth century, under the kings Ahab, Jehoram, and Jehu. The prophets lived in the outskirts of the country with some of the poorest people of the nation.

hospitality through Elisha brought her and her children salvation from starvation and from slavery. This hospitality was not an abstract economic decision; Elisha peered into the faces of the needy and saw the act of mercy that he must perform. Though the laws demanded that widows and orphans such as these must receive the care and attention of the whole people, such structural mechanisms for social justice often fail in practice. In such cases, personal intervention alone can bring God's salvation to the needy and forgotten.

Elijah and Elisha both intervened on behalf of the needy. Their miracles provided enough food to eat and enough money to keep the creditors at bay. Those whom they have helped receive a bounty that is shared with others. The help never makes anyone wealthy, but it always makes them rich enough to share. Like oil pouring from one jug to another, wealth can never be accumulated, but only shared from one person to another.

Elisha also receives the care and provision of others. Because he has never accumulated wealth while providing for others, there are times that he has need of provision by others. He accepts help from the wealthy so that their wealth keeps flowing, as well.

> One day Elisha was passing through Shunem, where a wealthy woman lived, who prevailed upon him to eat a meal. So whenever he passed that way, he would stop there for a meal. She said to her husband, "I know that this man who passes through here is a holy man of God. Let us make a small roof chamber with walls, and put there for him a bed, a table, a chair, and a lamp, and he will stay there whenever he comes to us."
>
> 2 Kings 4:8–10

The woman provides housing for Elisha out of her own wealth. But later, Elisha discusses this with his companion, Gehazi. Wealth must keep flowing, they understand, so what can they give to this woman who gives to them? At first, Elisha considers the possible benefits of his political connections, but the woman insists that she has no need of such things. But Elisha and Gehazi keep thinking about this. Wealth *must* keep flowing![7] Then Gehazi has an idea. She has no son and her

---

[7] The metaphor of flowing wealth begins to sound like political "trickle-down" theories. Of course, such politics tend to credit rich people as being the source of wealth, usurping the place rightfully

husband is old. So Elisha announces to her that she will have a son within a year. Although she is incredulous, this gift comes to her as a miracle and she rejoices with the new kind of wealth that she experiences in her son. A life of rejoicing about miracles, however, does not guarantee a life without tragedy.

> When the child was growing up, he went out one day to his father among the reapers. He said to his father, "My head, my head!" The father said to his servant, "Carry him to his mother." The servant carried him and brought him to his mother; the child sat on her lap until noon, and he died. She went up and laid him on the bed of the man of God. Then she shut the door and went out.
>
> 2 Kings 4:18–21

If the story ended here, then there would be a clear consistency with the theme presented before. Wealth must keep flowing, and here we reach the terrible conclusion to the truth: Even the wealth of a son must leave someday. But the story insists on a slightly different truth: We must always be willing to give up our wealth and to give it away. In the end, wealth belongs only to God, not to the persons who share it for a little while.[8] The Shunammite woman takes the body of her dead son and places it on Elisha's bed.

Elisha is not there, however; he is in another part of the country taking care of others. The woman is not passive. She knows what must be done to save her child and she sets forth to do it. She refuses to tell her husband about their son's death. Instead, she simply says, "It will be all right." Then she takes a donkey and a servant and goes to seek Elisha. At first, Elisha sends Gehazi back to the boy, sending along his staff to lay upon the boy to bring him back to life. When this attempted miracle

---

belonging to God; thus, these plans tend to be idolatrous. Also, if the government has received wealth, it must distribute the wealth, against the plans of many "trickle-down" theorists. At root, two problems plague the "trickle-down" theories. Firstly, the political theories do not take into account the sinful human urge to hoard goods rather than allow the wealth to flow. Secondly, the wealth must not trickle down one drip at a time; wealth must gush with such force that people get carried away by their will to give.

[8] This is the church's classic understanding of stewardship. God owns all wealth and possessions; people serve for a while as stewards of part of this wealth.

fails and the boy remains dead, Elisha has to go himself. When he arrives, he lies on the boy and breathes life back into him.

Faith and hospitality lead to each other. Because the woman believed that Elisha was a holy servant of God, she provided housing for the prophet. Because she had been hospitable and had seen the results of provision, she could say in faith that everything was all right, even when she had just watched her child die in her arms. Because of her faith in Elisha's miracles, the prophet could resurrect her son in another miracle of hospitality. Too often, the modern church tries to separate religion from provision, faith from justice. God's prophets, however, see the connection intimately and know that either one, done fully in God's name, leads inevitably to the other.

Elisha's many other miracles continue to express God's hospitality toward those in need. Disease was a problem that Elisha addressed repeatedly. The stories of these miracles are charming tales of how God and Elisha together keep the people safe from every kind of harm.

> When Elisha returned to Gilgal, there was a famine in the land. As the company of prophets was sitting before him, he said to his servant, "Put the large pot on, and make some stew for the company of the prophets." One of them went out into the field to gather herbs, and he found a wild vine and gathered from it a lapful of wild gourds, and came and cut them up into the pot of stew, but no one knew. They ladled some for the men to eat. But while they were eating the stew, they cried out, "O man of God, there is death in the pot!" They could not continue eating. He said, "Bring some flour." He threw it into the pot, and said, "Pour some for the people and let them eat." And there was nothing harmful in the pot.
>
> 2 Kings 4:38–41

Problems with food are a concern for God's people. Safety in drinking water and in all the things that people eat must be addressed. Every person must have food that brings health, and the responsibility for assuring this belongs to God's people. Of course, quantity as well as quality receives attention.

> A man came from Baal-shalishah, bringing food from the first fruits to the man of God: twenty loaves of barley and fresh ears of grain in his sack. Elisha said, "Give it to the

people and let them eat." But his assistant said, "How can I set this before a hundred people?" So he repeated, "Give it to the people and let them eat, for thus says Yahweh, 'They shall eat and have some left.'" He set it before them, they ate, and had some left, according to the word of Yahweh.

2 Kings 4:42–44

In one of the church's favorite stories about Jesus, the feeding of the five thousand, a tiny bit of food miraculously increases to provide an adequate meal for thousands. Such stories did not begin with Jesus, but had been part of God's activity with the people for nearly a thousand years by Jesus' time. God's commands have always been that people should provide enough food for everyone in the community. When God provides food, there is plenty for all who need to eat. At times this adequate provision fails. Because of human sin, the plates of some lack food. When God's prophets, or even the church today, see that hunger face to face, there remains no choice but to provide for those who lack. Such is the nature of the hospitality that God has ordained from the beginning.

Jesus' Hospitality

Jesus' ministry exhibited the kind of hospitality that the law and the prophets had championed. Many episodes recorded in the Gospels detail how Jesus fed the hungry, healed the sick, and showed kindness to those who were rejected.[9] A full discussion of these texts showing Jesus' compassionate and active hospitality would constitute a book by itself. However, one passage must receive consideration.

For some people, "hospitality" means returning favors. One friend invites another to dinner; then the second friend returns the favor. I go to a friend's house, and then I invite the friend to my house. Everything is even, in the long run. This equality of giving is honorable, to be sure, but hospitality is much more than reciprocity. Hospitality gives to those who cannot give back, as Jesus was constantly reminding his followers.

---

[9] Jesus also commanded others to take these actions in God's name (Matthew 25:31–46).

Jesus said to one who had invited him, "When you provide a lunch or a dinner, do not call your friends, or your brothers, or your sisters, or your relatives, or your wealthy neighbors. They would only invite you back, and you would be repaid. Instead, when you throw a party, invite the poor, the crippled, the lame, and the blind. Then you will be happy, because they cannot repay you. You will be repaid at the resurrection of the righteous."

Luke 14:12-14

For Jesus, hospitality means giving with no expectation of return. In fact, hospitality is when you give with no possibility of any return. This makes sure that there will be true hospitality, because wealth will flow. If you give to those who can give back, wealth never really flows; it stagnates. Like waves in a small brackish pool, the wealth washes on one side, and then on the next, and back and forth in quick succession, but the wealth never really gets anywhere. This is not hospitality at all, but only self-gratification. Immediately, Jesus offered a parable, to help the hearers understand this.

A certain man provided a great dinner, and he invited many people. He sent his servant when it was time for the dinner, to say to those who were invited: "Come! It's ready already." But everyone alike began to decline the invitations. The first one said to him, "I just bought a field, and I need to go out to it and look it over. I ask you to accept my regrets." Another one said, "I bought some yokes of oxen—five of them—and I'm going to test them. I ask you to accept my regrets." Another one said, "I just got married; that's why I am not able to come."

The servant went back and told his master these things. Then the ruler of the house was angry, and he said to his servant, "Go quickly into the streets and alleys of the city and bring in here the poor, and the crippled, and the blind, and the lame." The servant said, "Master, what you have ordered has been done, and there is still room." The master said to the servant, "Go into the roads and the lanes; they must come in, so that my house is full. I tell you that not one of those who were invited will taste my dinner."

Luke 14:16–24

This parable emphasizes the need to share God's wealth. This one person, a king, had nearly endless amounts of wealth, but refused to hoard them. Wealth must flow freely. Even when the king's friends did not wish to join the party where the king's wealth would flow to them, the wealth must flow. Those who reject God's banquet, at which God's wealth is shared, are themselves rejected. Everyone must share in the flow of wealth from God through people to others. Destruction awaits those who do not allow wealth to flow.

Despite the king's bitter disappointment in his friends, the wealth must flow, so the servants went out to find new guests for the joyous banquet. Someone must share the wealth, so the servants looked for people who would gladly accept what the king freely wished to give. The street people, those who were poorest, received the invitation and accepted it with glee. They understood the proper response to the king's invitation and to God's graciousness.[10] All must do their part in wealth's continual flowing. Some must give and some must accept, only to pass it on later. Wealth cannot flow without all doing their own parts.

The Church's Hospitality

For the early church, hospitality was an essential element of the sacrament of communion. Communion demonstrated the oneness of God's people, who were united by their common ties around the table of God. The early church concerned itself deeply with economic needs. Paul's churches took offerings to help the needy believers in the Palestinian churches.[11] The book of Acts records the early church's efforts to provide equitably for needy persons.[12] The poor served as a constant object of the early Christian church's active compassion.

Problems with the distribution of wealth existed within the church as well. As the church grew, there became an increas-

---

[10] Bernard Brandon Scott, *Hear Then the Parable: A Commentary on the Parables of Jesus* (Minneapolis: Fortress Press, 1989), pp. 161-163, notes that those who accept the invitation to the dinner are those who enter into the kingdom of God.

[11] See Romans 15:25–29; 1 Corinthians 16:1–4; and 2 Corinthians 8—9.

[12] Acts 6:1–4.

ingly wide variety of persons involved. The difference between the
rich and the poor grew at the same time, resulting in the possibility
of divisions within the churches. Paul's attempts to keep all the
church's participants together were not always successful, so at
times he spoke harshly with those who were being inhospitable:

> Now in these instructions I am not approving, because
> when you come together it is not for the better but for the
> worse. Firstly, when you come together into a church, I
> hear that there are divisions among you, and partly I
> believe it. Indeed, there even have to be factions among
> you, so that the "genuine" among you can become known.
> When you come together, it is not really to eat the Lord's
> supper. Each of you goes ahead with the eating of your own
> supper, and one goes hungry and another becomes drunk.
> What! Do you not have homes in which to eat and drink?
> Would you rather despise the church of God and humiliate
> those who have nothing? What should I say to you? Should
> I approve you? In this I do not approve!
>
> 1 Corinthians 11:17–22

Paul's severe speech is striking. He accuses the richer
believers with showing contempt for the church of God. One can
be certain that the rich people did not understand themselves
in that way! Instead, they probably saw themselves as merely
trying to preserve what they already had. They were not trying
to take what rightly belonged to others; they just wanted to enjoy
what they had worked so hard to have.

Their attitudes are difficult for the modern church to con-
demn. However, Paul's own condemnation is harsh. These rich
persons were more interested in preserving their wealth and in
maintaining the status quo than they were committed to following Christ's principles of hospitality toward others. This hospitality inevitably means that wealth must flow; it must not be
hoarded. The rich Corinthian Christians wanted to share their
food around the table with those who already had enough to eat,
but wealth must flow to those who do not have enough.

By resisting the notion of hospitality, these Christians violated the communion. They turned the elements of the Lord's
Supper into mere food and drink, removing all notions of a
sacramental observance of Jesus' life and death. Their actions
provide a lesson for the church today: When economics are
absent from the communion table, it is not the Lord's Supper.

The lesson is clear: The table must be a place of healing and restoration, not division. The table must share the wealth of the church, not hoard it.[13] Economic fairness and communal togetherness cannot be separated. The church's true business is to provide for each other and for others; in doing so, the church expresses its giving nature to the world.

> Awe came upon everyone, because many wonders and signs were being done by the apostles. All who believed were as one and had all things together. They were selling their possessions and goods and distributing the proceeds to all, as any had need. Each day, as they spent much time together in the temple, they broke bread at home and shared their food with joyful and simple hearts, praising God and having goodwill among all the people. Each day the Lord added to their number those who were being saved.
>
> Acts 2:43-47

The early church shared their possessions to care for human needs and shared communion with each other. This was the pattern set by the early church, and this pattern is still useful today. Furthermore, this pattern brought about opportunities for growth within the church, as salvation pours forth through God's church. Evangelism and social justice must never be opposites in the church's vocabulary; when that happens, the church ceases to be the church.

Answering the Call to the Table

God calls people to the communion table. The call goes forth around the earth, far and wide. Millions respond, but millions more cannot hear the call over the shouts of their own

---

[13]I question, therefore, the practice of some churches of collecting the offering and then placing it on the communion table for the remainder of the service. This is often accompanied by persons who bring the offering forward, after it is collected, while others pray for God's blessings and sanctification over these funds. The imagery seems backward. The church's task is not the collection of funds, but the dispersion of funds. The offering should be collected and then ceremonially sent out from the sanctuary into the world where service and sharing take place. Wealth must flow; it must not be hoarded, even by the church on the table of communion.

starving stomachs. Whole nations perceive of Christians as the foreign exploiters who take from them, never giving anything back and rarely leaving even the opportunity for continued life. This tragic vision of the church must be replaced by a vision of the church's hospitality. Truly, the church has been called to hospitality by God since the beginning of God's involvement with people. Hospitality means letting the wealth flow until it meets the needs of hunger, thirst, security, shelter, and solidarity. Hospitality is not an option for the church; it is God's option for all people.

When we gather around the table, we partake of tokens of bread and wine that are themselves tokens of Christ's body and blood. We can come to the table in answer to God's call because we have already partaken of more than tokens. We already have had enough to eat at home that we can come to the table. For others, tokens of food are not enough because they do not have enough to eat and drink. It is a cruel trick to call them to the table for only a fraction of a square inch of flat bread and a portion of an ounce of juice. Those of us who have enough to eat must remember to heed our call as well, which is a call to make a world where there is no hunger. God gives us our wealth so that it can flow out to others and provide for their needs, before they reach the table hungry.

God's call to communion and to hospitality should echo in our ears each time we approach the table. Likewise, we should repeat to ourselves Paul's warning: If we partake of the tokens before others have more than tokens, it is not the Lord's Supper that we eat.

7

the moral community

Deep within me are ingrained many rules of social behavior. These rules cover almost every social interaction I ever have, from hellos to good-byes, from which things must be done in public to which must be done in private, from where to sleep (not in public, except sometimes on airplanes) to where to comb my hair (never at a meal table) to what bodily noises are appropriate in public (almost none—but some require an "Excuse me" and some are better to ignore completely). Sometimes the rules get too complex to remember. I have managed to figure out where to put the silverware and which one to use when, unless there's more than five or six utensils. At weddings, one should say "Congratulations" to the groom and "Best wishes" to the bride—or maybe it's the other way around. That one always confused me, so I usually just mumble something.

One of these rules of etiquette has stuck with me from my youth, and I hardly ever break it—don't be the first one to eat. Watch to see what everyone else does first, and copy them. It can save a lot of embarrassment. In particular, it can save the embarrassment of having a mouth full of food when someone else says, "Let us pray." Of course, my rule about not going first can cause some awkwardness, too, as we all sit around the table waiting for someone else to go first.

Different people have different rules about "saying grace." The rule can be "always" or "never"; "only at home" or "only at restaurants"; "the youngest prays" or "the oldest prays" or "the one who pays prays"; "men do all the praying" or "women do all

the praying" or "everyone takes a turn." With all the different
rules, "saying grace" gets confusing, but I think most of the
time, the rules boil down to two: "We pray if there's a minister
watching" and "we pray for 'special' meals." The phrase *special
meals* still confuses me. Which meals are "special"? Any meal?
Any meal with friends? Any meal with family? Any meal with
people you haven't seen for a long time? Only Christmas and
Thanksgiving? What does it take to make a meal special?

One thing is certain: Communion is a special meal. It is not
just any old combination of food and family; it is special and it
definitely follows a prayer (or several). A congregation may eat
many meals together, such as socials and potlucks, but communion is different. Even if a church dinner includes prayers,
songs, a speaker, and an offering, it's still not the same as
communion.

What makes communion special? Chapter 5 emphasized
the joyous nature of communion. Certainly, it is a meal of
communal solidarity. Together, God's people rejoice and celebrate their togetherness. In chapter 6, communion addressed
the problem of hoarded wealth. Oppression and subjugation
have no place at God's table. All approach the table as equals
and wealth flows among them, never stopping for long anywhere. Communion, though, is more than a celebration and it
is more than sharing, as important as those elements are.

Communion is a meal partaken in memory of Christ.[1] Thus
the community that communion forms is distinct from communities formed in worship of other deities. Christ makes communion special and sets forth the nature of the meal. More than
celebration and sharing, communion forms identity. Because of
Jesus, we celebrate and we share when we partake of communion,
since that way of life is what Jesus taught, just as the Old Testament
had taught it before. The people who gather around the communion table are unmistakably Christ's people. There can be no other
god than the God of Jesus whom we have worshiped through both
Old and New Testaments.

Communion is a practice against idolatry. It keeps everyone's
mind and heart focused on the real reason for communion:

---

[1] This is the central issue in *Baptism, Eucharist and Ministry* (Faith
and Order Paper 111; Geneva: World Council of Churches, 1982), pp.
10–12.

Jesus Christ. Other gods than the one true God have no room at this table. The bread and the wine commit us to Jesus and warn us away from any competitors. Food alone does not make communion, nor does celebration and sharing, nor even the presence of a god—only Jesus and the God of Christ make communion special.

Idolatrous Food

In ancient times, meat was scarce. Any meal with meat was a special occasion. Such meals tended to be large events, involving many people from throughout the community. Extended families and groups of friends would join in the meal, or perhaps co-workers and other associates would participate. Meat was a party food, and any meal with meat was usually a big party.

Many of these big parties were held at temples. A temple in the Greek and Roman world during the church's earliest years would have offered a wide range of services for these kinds of parties. There would be a room large enough for all the guests, a kitchen big enough to prepare the food, and a willing and experienced butcher and chef, called the priest. The temple itself sponsored many meals around its own schedule of religious holidays, but other people could use the temple facilities for their own, secular parties.[2] Even in these other parties, a pagan priest was in the kitchen, offering the meat as a sacrifice to some other god.

For early Christians, these parties at temples caused problems. Of course, one should not attend the pagan temples' official religious observances, but what about the parties thrown by one's own friends? Did Christians have to give up the meat they were being offered? Such proved to be difficult and controversial problems for the early Christians, just as similar practices of meals had been problems for God's followers throughout Old Testament times. Food offered to idols has always been a powerful temptation.

---

[2] For more information on the use of temples for secular parties, see Dennis E. Smith and Hal E. Taussig, *Many Tables: The Eucharist in the New Testament and Liturgy Today* (Philadelphia: Trinity Press International, 1990), pp. 21–35.

Idolatrous food tempts because it is physically good. God designed our bodies to enjoy food, and that enjoyment was not limited by the faith of the one preparing the food. The meat sacrificed to idols was the same kind of meat as religiously pure food. It came from the same kind of animals and was prepared in much the same way. The aroma of idolatrous food was just as savory and the taste was just as mouth-watering. The company around the table may not have been someone's "church friends," but they were good folk from the town anyway. The pagan temples were not sleazy joints in ill repair; they were in the best parts of town and were often the fancy places where the important people loved to eat. Those meals of idolatrous food had many things in their favor.

The problem was that the food had been consecrated in the service of some other god. The food was idolatrous. Sure, the food was just as sanitary. Sure, it tasted fine. Sure, everyone else was eating there—it was the place to be. All those favorable things, though, never quite removed the problem.

In modern times, these problems simply do not exist, and so it becomes hard for us to understand the biblical worryings about meat sacrificed to idols. Instead of problems with food sacrificed to idols, we moderns have problems because we have made our food into an idol.

We live in an age and a nation of gluttony. Food is good only when there is plenty of it. One never stops eating when one is full; our biggest national celebrations are in honor of bounty, and so each worshiper at these idolatrous tables of Thanksgiving and Christmas, as well as other such holidays, must eat until stuffed. God's sufficiency, so evident in communion, is abandoned in our longing for abundance. We worship our own stomachs and honor them with gifts of bountiful food.

Instead of wealth flowing, our special meals become a time of hoarding. Although a small token might be sent out as a holiday basket to some needy persons, the real feast is spread on our own tables. Relatives gather from distances and everyone works to "make sure there's enough to go around." Many times, the persons gathering for the meal would never consider spreading their goods outside their own circles. For all of us, our concerns center on ourselves. We make sure there's enough for us, and if that means that others in the world starve, it never even reaches our attention. Perhaps a short prayer at the start of the feast will mention briefly some of the world's needs, but these thoughts pass quickly. Wealth must flow, as we are taught by God's concerns with the economic welfare of the whole world, but instead our thoughts and actions point inexorably inward.

The proof of our idolatry is all around us, though we refuse to see it. Parents teach children to observe silence and decorum around the dinner table, just as young ones hear the admonishings not to run or laugh or chew gum in church. Silence and solemnity mark both the table of the home and the table of God, and so the two become confused. In the midst of that silence, it is hard to hear the laughter of the celebration that Christ intends.

The issue in silence and in gluttony is the same: control. In our meals, we want to exercise control over our part of the world. We choose what we eat and with whom we eat it; almost always our choices are for an overindulgence of food to be eaten with people just like us. The voices and sounds must be controlled, just as traditions govern so many of the actions at our special meals. If we were to face the truth, the control is only a symptom of an even worse problem: greed. We wish control to protect ourselves and to perpetuate selfishness. This kind of control leads only to gluttony and robs our ability to experience a joyous celebration of sharing.

A frightening question comes to mind: Do we treat communion that way? Has the church made its celebration of sharing into a controlled sacrament of selfishness? Too often, the answer has been yes. The church has transformed communion into an act of control. God's free gift of eucharist has been treated as a test of faith and used to keep people away from God. Communion has been proclaimed as something too good for ordinary people, and so religious practitioners of every age have appointed themselves as communion's protectors. The self-righteous strive to save God from the people, and in so doing they miss the whole point of communion, which God gives freely to save the people. Control does not belong with communion, even if the control is performed by those who appear religiously righteous and pure.

Notions of control have gone hand in hand with an emphasis on guilt. Feelings of guilt among God's people have been a prime tool of control. Time after time, when the people feel sufficiently guilty, those who exalt themselves can take advantage and gain control. Communion serves only as a pawn, to be

meted out in exchange for admissions of guilt and for acceptance of someone else's control. Greed lurks behind all of this.
The people become greedy for forgiveness and will do anything,
no matter what the cost, to receive a few words of assurance.
The controllers become greedy for even more control, and they
will subjugate anyone in God's name in order to protect and
enhance their own position. Walls are built around God's table,
and thick doors are placed in those walls. Controllers stand
guard at those gates, daring others to enter. But the true
meaning of the table is lost.

Idolatrous meals are a constant risk for persons of faith. The
seduction of a free meal that honors another god keeps
presenting itself to us, and often we feel the temptation. The
possibility of turning our meals, even communion, into selfish
acts of control keeps haunting us. Food so quickly becomes
idolatrous and gatherings become spoiled with hardly any
notice. The biblical injunctions against idolatrous food are
meaningful for us today, as well as to the ancient persons of faith
who have gone before us. Ezekiel and Paul both discuss what
to do with idolatrous meals.

In one sense, the answer has already been placed before us.
Communion is the answer to idolatrous meals. Communion is
a special meal not because of the celebration or because of the
sharing of wealth. It is not special because of those who are
around the table looking for food or because of its "religious"
nature. It is not special because of the history behind it or even the
ancient Christ events that originated the service of this table.
Communion is a special meal because of Jesus, with whom we eat.
With the God of Jesus Christ at the table, no room is available for
idols or for any other gods. Eating with Jesus makes the meal
special, because Jesus insists our devotion be toward the one God
alone. Jesus' presence at the table prevents idolatry, not through
any magical means but because loyalty is demanded and energized by God's being near.

Ezekiel and Individual Morality

The saying goes "You are what you eat." How true that is
when God's food is served at the table, but it is just as true when
other gods serve their suppers. When someone eats right, it
shows through all of life, but poor (spiritual) nutrition is just as
apparent. The prophet Ezekiel condemned those who ate the

wrong food. Although eating the wrong food was not bad in and of itself, it always led to worse things. In Ezekiel's days, God met with the people on the banks of rivers, but the other gods served their dinners on the mountains. The people flocked to the mountains to worship other gods around their dinner tables, and Ezekiel understood that their partaking of idolatrous food was the same as participating in a host of other problems.[3]

> If one is righteous and does what is lawful and right—
> if one does not eat upon the mountains,
> if one does not lift up the eyes to the idols of the house
>   of Israel,
> if one does not violate a neighbor's marriage,
> if one does not approach another for illicit sexual
>   behavior,
> if one does not oppress anyone and restores the pledge
>   to a debtor,
> if one does not commit robbery, but gives bread to
>   the hungry and covers the naked with a garment,
> if one does not accept advance interest,
> if one does not take accrued interest,
> but if one withholds the hand from iniquity,
> if one does truth and justice between people,
> if one follows my statutes,
> if one keeps my judgments to perform truth—
> such a one is righteous;
> such a one shall surely live,
> says the Lord Yahweh.
>   Ezekiel 18:6–9

This prohibition against participating in pagan meals denounces idolatry of all sorts, such as worship of pagan gods, adultery, oppression, robbery, and greediness. For Ezekiel, there is little difference between these various forms of idolatry.

First of all, Ezekiel forbids the eating of food on the mountains and the consideration of idols. These are two forms of the same problem of idolatry's perversion of the religious life. The mountains were the usual site for the worship of the fertility

---

[3] See Walter Harrelson, *The Ten Commandments and Human Rights* (Philadelphia: Fortress Press, 1980), p. 37; and John G. Gammie, *Holiness in Israel* (Minneapolis: Fortress Press, 1989), pp. 50–51.

gods of Canaan and other lands, so the prohibition of that sort of eating was a ban on participating in the worship of those other gods. Likewise, even the worship of Israelite idols was wrong. Unlike what certain others had said before him, Ezekiel is convinced that nationality has nothing to do with religion. Whether the pagan gods are foreign or not, there should still be no worship of them. The use of religion for well-being, for fertility, for nationalism, or for any kind of power was strictly against Ezekiel's religion. Righteousness for this prophet means the rejection of any schemes to bring personal benefit. Greed and control must be avoided.

Ezekiel's next focus concerns the proper treatment of women. Again, there should be no attempts toward personal gain. For the men to whom Ezekiel first spoke, it was forbidden to make anyone unclean, according to the ancient laws of ritual purity. A man should not make any woman unclean. Although this can refer to adulterous sexual relations, the text is ambiguous; it can refer to any time of ritual impurity. Impurity could result from a wide number of situations that made one temporarily unfit to be active in the religious services as well as in various parts of society. When impurity occurred, as it did for everyone from time to time, there were prescribed methods for purification. Often, this restoring of purity required time alone, perhaps in prayer and meditation. In the time of ancient Israel, women were less protected by the law, but Ezekiel deals with this lack of safety. The prophet commands the people to be careful around the disadvantaged, especially women who have received lesser positions in society because of their gender. All persons should take special care not to bring impurity upon these disadvantaged ones or to interrupt their processes of restoring purity. The goal for the society as a whole is clear: Purity must be enhanced.

The topic turns to more typical prophetic concerns. The last forbidden act is a general one: any type of oppression against any sort of person. The word used here for oppression echoes what happened to the Israelites while they were slaves in Egypt before the Exodus. Exodus 22:20 reminds the Israelites: "You should not oppress a resident alien or afflict one, since you were resident aliens in the nation of Egypt." Any type of greed or control would lead to oppression, and God charges the people with avoiding such acts. Instead, there are actions that should be done in order to oppose oppression.

When persons in ancient Israel incurred a debt, they were required to give their creditors a personal object as collateral. This custom fits into many of the Old Testament's stories, such as the objects that Tamar requires from Judah when he enters into her debt (Genesis 38:16–18). She requires Judah's signet, cord, and staff, all of which were necessary implements for maintaining authority and conducting business. Amos condemns those creditors who fail to care for the items they receive in pledge for debts (Amos 2:8). Those who give the pledge back to the debtor are acting rightly by refusing to oppress those who are economically disadvantaged.

The avoidance of robbery enters into another dimension of Israelite social responsibility. This term for robbery implies a forceful act of tearing; the closest English equivalent is a "rip-off." Robbery is an inherently violent act. It is a particularly active form of oppression. Ezekiel knows the many forms that greedy control can take. There are the quiet afflictions, when social structures, norms, and expectations are made to work to one's own advantage while depriving the needs of others. This type of economic violence is disruptive nonetheless. It is exemplified in the keeping of persons' pledges, which may well have been considered acceptable by much of society, as well as in other actions found further down in the list: taking interest on loans. Ezekiel condemns these "passive" oppressions, but also emphasizes a ban against the more active forms, such as forceful seizure or robbery, and also the exercise of power for wickedness. When one stretches forth the hand, it implies a power, whether physical or otherwise; Ezekiel commands that one's hand or power be restrained. Violence and power, just like any other form of greed and control, are the opposite of what God wants from the people.

God's desires are made even more clear at the end of the list. Four items appear in quick succession: bringing true justice, walking in God's statutes, keeping God's judgments, and doing truth. God's statutes are to be taken with utmost seriousness. The divinely given laws are not arbitrary; they are not hoops through which we should jump without rhyme or reason. Instead, God has instructed the people with great specificity about the type of society that God desires. Truth and justice are foremost qualities in this society, and the commands and laws are steps along this path that God would have us follow. God's people should observe all of God's instructions, so that this vision of society can be brought into its fullness. Such is the path of righteousness, and those who walk in these paths shall live.

For Ezekiel, each individual is responsible for these acts of justice. This idea is not at all unusual for us, since we are used to thinking that salvation comes only as a result of the faith expressed by an individual person. The ancient Israelites, however, thought differently. They had seen that God had worked among them as a nation, and the greatest saving acts (such as the Exodus) had been done for the people as a whole. God does not save only a few based on merit, but the whole nation. If not the whole nation, then God's salvation at least deals with more than one person at a time. The Israelites knew about the interconnectedness of God's creation, and they felt blessing—as well as cursing—coming to groups of people, not to individuals alone. This interconnectedness found expression in one of the greatest statements of God's nature, as God proclaimed to Moses:

> Yahweh,
> Yahweh,
> God of compassion and mercy,
> > slow to anger,
> > abundant in loyalty and truth,
> preserving loyalty for thousands,
> > taking away iniquity and sin,
> who will in no way consider innocent the guilty,
> > pursuing the iniquity of the ancestors
> > upon the children and the grandchildren,
> > to the third and the fourth generations.
> > > Exodus 34:6–7

In this ancient expression of faith, God is concerned with creating and protecting the right society. That concerns extends to such a degree that God will seek out iniquity, even into the subsequent generations. Problems must be rooted out of people, and God is very active in this process. God is no laissez-faire deity, but energetically attacks problems until they are solved. Although the talk of visiting iniquities of the ancestors upon the generations sounds negative to our ears, to the ancients it would have been the perfect expression of God's loyalty and loving care, because God's continuing activity means the gradual improvement of the world.

This faith found its way into the Old Testament in many ways, including one interesting proverb that is found twice in almost identical words (Jeremiah 31:29 and Ezekiel 18:2):

> The ancestors have eaten unripened grapes;
> and the descendants' teeth become numb.

The sense of this strange-sounding proverb is clear: When the ancestors do something, the descendants feel the effects. This expresses the same faith about God's activity in the world as found in Exodus 34: God keeps working to solve the long-standing, multigenerational problems that pervade society. In such a world, communal responsibility receives the emphasis. Each person is responsible for everyone else. When one acts, others feel the effects. This kind of mutuality is now being rediscovered in many ways, such as the contemporary ecological movement. This faith of ancient Israel communicates a timeless truth of everyone's responsibility for all of God's creation.

Both Jeremiah and Ezekiel reject this proverb, however. They sense a danger in communal responsibility, and they speak a new word of God in order to fix the problems they have found.

> The word of Yahweh came to me, saying: "Why are you speaking this proverb about the land of Israel, saying, 'The ancestors have eaten unripened grapes; and the descendants' teeth become numb'? As I live," an utterance of Lord Yahweh, "let this proverb never again be spoken in Israel. All souls belong to me. The soul of an ancestor is just like the soul of a descendant. They belong to me. The soul that sins will die."
>
> Ezekiel 18:1–4

Even as the faith of Exodus 34 seemed harsh to us, this statement of a correction to that faith seems harsh. In Ezekiel's portrait, the one who sins will be held responsible for that sin, even to the point of death. Individual responsibility replaces the old, rejected idea of communal responsibility. Yet, it hardly seems that the two ideas are in complete disagreement, or that the prophet entirely desires the abandonment of communal responsibility. The situation seems more complicated than that.

Ezekiel sees deep problems with communal responsibility. When the whole group is responsible, one may tend to negate the importance of one's own actions. If each generation lives the situation deserved by its parents, then perhaps nothing can be done to change things for the better. If communal responsibility is understood in this fashion, perhaps there is no reason to do what is right. Everything that happens is always someone else's fault, and so correcting it must be someone else's problem, if anything can be done about it at all. Against these ideas, Ezekiel reemphasizes the other part of the issue: individual responsibility.

Each individual person is responsible for accepting and maintaining the morality of the faith. For Ezekiel, the burden cannot be passed to any other shoulders. This emphasis on the individual corrects the central position of the community in most of Israelite faith without rejecting it. Each person's actions impact the whole society, and so the community is responsible for itself and each person is responsible for all others. Individuals share the responsibility with the community.

For Ezekiel, this whole issue of individual responsibility ties into the importance of where one eats. The changed proverb in Ezekiel 18:1–4 moves directly into the commands for morality in 18:5-9. Each is responsible for her or his own actions, and that means that no one should be allowed to eat the meals of other gods. Participation in those meals is an acceptance of a pagan system of belief, and that leaves the God of the ancient faith outside of one's life. Proper worship cannot be separated from proper morality, and the actions of the individual cannot be separated from the effects of those actions upon the whole community. The purposes of God require worship *and* morality, individual loyalty *and* communal solidarity.

Such connections are the same in the church of today. Morality among individuals is essential to the community's morality. True communion calls the community—and each individual within it—to higher morality, because of the God whom we meet around that table.

Paul and Community Responsibility

The issue of meals for other gods did not disappear after Ezekiel's proclamations. Early in the church's life, the apostle Paul dealt with these same issues.

> Concerning food offered to idols, we know that "there are no idols in the world," and that "there is no God but one." Indeed, even though there may be so-called gods in heaven or on earth—as in fact there are many gods

and many lords—yet for us there is one God, the Father,
from whom are all things and for whom we exist, and
one Lord, Jesus Christ, through whom are all things and
through whom we exist.

1 Corinthians 8:4–6

Paul recognizes the problem and then launches immediately into a theological discussion of idols. According to Paul,
idols have no existence. They are not real. Thus, they can have
no effect upon the worshiper. Paul's argument is much more
legalistic and philosophical than Ezekiel's treatment of the
same topic. Ezekiel discusses the things that God's people
should do, in contrast to the actions of those who eat idolatrous
food. The prophet offers important insights into the nature of
idolatry: It is more than the worship of other gods: It includes the
morality that accompanies false worship. Greed and an impulse
toward control are the essence of idolatry, and this kind of
idolatry contradicts the God of the Bible, who provides sufficiently instead of abundantly and who struggles to be surprising,
not controllable. Ezekiel institutes an individual morality: Each
one must be careful not to participate in idolatry of any sort.

Paul works much differently. Because idols are nothing, there
is no need to decide what to do when idols are involved. Food is
just food and it makes no difference upon whose altar the food has
been cooked. Anyone who knows this can partake of any kind of
food with no danger at all. Paul argues against magic and against
any interpretation of idolatrous food—or communion, for that
matter—that emphasizes a miraculous nature within the food
itself. Those who realize the truth about idols can eat that meat in
clear conscience, but for Paul, that leads to a deeper problem.

But not everyone has this knowledge. Some are presently
accustomed to idols, and they still think of the food they eat
as food offered to an idol; and their conscience, being
weak, is defiled. "Food will not bring us close to God." We
are no worse off if we do not eat, and no better off if we do.

1 Corinthians 8:7–8

Not everyone knows that idols are nothingness. Many of the
Christians in the early Corinthian church had been pagans and had
believed fervently in the saving power of the food of their gods.
Having rejected their earlier pagan religion, they feel now that all
should avoid the food that was the essence of those non-Christian

religions. Paul virtually dismisses this argument, for the time being. There is nothing in the idol meat itself that makes anyone any better or any worse. Paul, then, accepts Ezekiel's emphasis on individual responsibility for morality, but applies this principle in a strikingly different way. Whereas Ezekiel felt no one should eat idolatrous food, Paul sees no problem with it, and encourages people to do whatever they want.

Paul's concerns quickly leave the abstract level, however. He moves to a discussion of the conflict between people that this theological problem has created:

> Watch that all your liberty does not somehow become a stumbling block to the weak. For if others see you, with knowledge, sitting at the table in the worship of an idol, might they not, since their conscience is weak, be encouraged to the point of eating food sacrificed to idols? Thus by your knowledge those weak believers for whom Christ died are destroyed. But when you thus sin against members of your family, and wound their conscience when it is weak, you sin against Christ. Therefore, if food is a cause of their falling, I will never eat meat, so that I may not cause one of them to fall.
>
> 1 Corinthians 8:9–13

Paul's understanding of individual responsibility in moral issues has given every Christian the liberty to choose their moral activity for themselves. It is almost that each Christian can decide what is moral and what is not. Ezekiel surely could not have agreed with this position, since that prophet had a much clearer statement of what was right and wrong.

But Paul does not stop with the emphasis in individual decision-making. Another factor is to be considered, namely, the effect one's individual moral decision has on others. The communal dimension re-enters the moral scene. Although it may not matter on an individual scale what decisions are made, on the communal level it is vital that persons work for *others'* individual morality. Only in this context does Paul use the word *sin* for those who eat the idolatrous food: "thus sinning against members of the family...you sin against Christ" (1 Corinthians 8:12). One's relationship to such objects as food does not matter, and even one's relationship to God is not what causes the act to become sin. Sin happens when people damage someone else's morality, and that becomes sin against Christ.

Paul constructs a principle for a new morality. Compared to Ezekiel, the results are the same: The eating of idolatrous food is not allowed. Paul and Ezekiel share the combination of individual and communal responsibility, but the combinations are a bit different. Ezekiel argues that each person must work for the morality of the community, but Paul insists that the whole community of faith must work to enhance the morality of each member, even and especially the disadvantaged ones. Paul does not base this new morality on self-purity, but on caring for all the others who gather around the table of God. We each must do what we can to support the morality of others.

Communion and Morality

The morality of the community participates in communion. The call to communion embodies God's desire for an ethical people. Looking around the table, God envisions the world that can be if God's people behave in obedience to God's continual instruction.

At the table, God's people remember that they have been invited to other tables, hosted by other gods. Idolatrous food abounds in this world and its enticing aromas have attracted all of us. Those who gather at God's table must resist those seductive smells and feast from the sufficient food of the one true God. Idols are nothing, as Paul rightly recognizes, but that rarely seems to stop humans from chasing after them.

At God's table, the people also remember the temptation to worship the food itself as our god. Like any other idol, it is made by our own hands. It embodies our ability to make our own way in the world. It pleases and satisfies. If we make our own food, we can control it and we can have it in abundance. If need be, we can keep others from having their share just so that we can grow fat on our hoard. God calls us to reject the idolatry of food.

God's people face further temptations. We can even start to worship God's sufficient, spiritual food that is offered at Christ's table. We can take the Gospel and parcel it out to those who so need it. We can distribute it (of course, we eschew the language of commerce, and prefer words like "evangelism") in tiny tastefuls that tantalize without nourishing. We can make up rules about who can partake of the sacred communion and we can draw those restrictive lines tight around us. We can turn God's gift into a sacrament, claiming that the food holds the power to change our lives, when in reality only the living God can truly transform us. We humans can act in such ways to turn the table of morality into deepest immorality. In the name of God, we can destroy the power of communion that God gives us; history shows us that we have succumbed to these temptations far too often. God's table is long and wide, and God shares the sufficient bread and the challenging wine with people who differ from us, even with some we call our enemies. If we were hosting the table, we would only invite a few people, people like us, people who can be trusted. That is why we must never claim to host the table. Only God hosts, and God invites all persons.

The table focuses on Christ. Only Christ reigns at this table. All the rest of us are merely guests, and that is more than enough for us. When the table focuses on Christ and when we sit around that table and focus ourselves on Christ, then we reject the immorality and the idolatry that can well up from our own souls. Christ as the table's centerpiece and Christ as the center of our lives keep us centered on morality and on what is truly sacred—every person among God's creation, throughout the world and throughout history.

Eucharist is a promise. In this sacred act and at this special meal, the community makes two promises. We promise, as individual persons, to seek the moral life and to dedicate ourselves to right action in this complicated and confusing world, because we know that our actions will impact the world and the community of faith, in the present and in the future. We promise, as a community, to support and enhance the morality of all of us, because we know that it is easy to stumble and that only the loving hands of the faith community can keep our feet steady on God's path.

Communion calls us, both the person and the community, to this kind of morality. Communion urges us toward a distinctive way of life in the world, in order to bring morality to the forefront of the world stage. Communion challenges the faith community into morality; the faith community should then challenge the world.

The table's focus on the one God keeps us resisting all the many forms of paganism that are found at other tables. Eating together brings us a solidarity. Communion is more than that solidarity, however, just as it is more than celebration and more than sharing wealth. It is more than just a meal, it is time with Christ—and the community needs nothing more to become the living example of and the clarion call to morality.

III

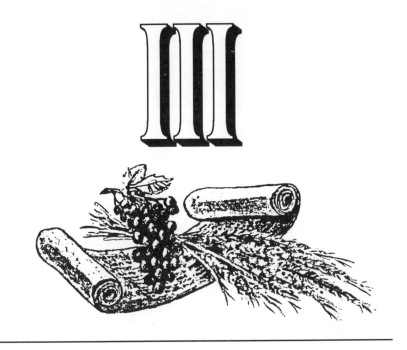

theology

8

the new covenant

I have vivid memories of communion meditations that I heard as a young child. Communion and its meaning were made crystal clear. There were two elements to the Lord's Supper: bread and wine. Of course, the "bread" consisted of pellets and the "wine" was watered-down grape juice, but we knew what the pastor meant anyway. The elements represented covenants. The bread was the Old Testament—dry, crusty, liable to stick in the throat. The wine was the New Testament—sweet, fragrant, pleasing. The bread reminded us of the old covenant, in which sin killed. None of us wanted the old covenant, but we had to have it in order to be ready for the new covenant. There was no reason why the old covenant was worth anything at all; it came first because God wanted it that way and we were in no place to question that. The wine was the blood of Jesus that bought for us the new covenant, in which we could have life abundant because of the power of the blood that now ran through us. Communion was a simple and sweet pairing of opposites: bread/wine, pellets/juice, Old Testament/New Testament, old covenant/new covenant, sin/salvation, death/life. How could it be any clearer?

Yet those early memories haunted me for years. God's inconsistency was bothersome—why should there ever have been an old covenant (and an Old Testament)? Why couldn't God have just started with the new covenant? Was the first a mistake? Did God first have to get the punishment over with before salvation could start? If God was truly unchanging, why an "old" and a "new" covenant? Can God's rich relationships with the world, which take so many different forms because of the varieties of human experience, truly be reduced to one short formula of a "new covenant"? As simple as those early communion meditations made it seem, things were never really that simple.

Communion functions as part of a new covenant. So the proper recognition and celebration of communion must take place within the context of thinking about that covenant. God's covenants in the Old Testament are far from irrelevant. To comprehend God's work with the people of this world, including the work celebrated around the communion table, one needs to understand the "old" and the "new" covenants. Such an understanding realizes that "old" and "new" are not so much enemies of each other, but instead two rich ways of saying the same thing—the full, dynamic message of God to the world.

Covenant as Obligation

Abraham

God's first partner in covenant was Abraham. The story of Abraham (who was named Abram at birth) begins rather suddenly.

> Yahweh said to Abram, "Go from your country, from your relatives, and from your family to the country that I will show you. I will make you into a large people; I will bless you and make your name great, and it will be a blessing. I will bless those who bless you, and the one who curses you will I curse. In you all the clans of the earth shall be blessed. So Abram went, as Yahweh told him.
>
> Genesis 12:1–4a

Such was the beginning of the relationship that God and Abraham had. They traveled together down a bumpy path, but the many obstacles and difficulties were overcome. This beginning was not particularly auspicious; in fact, its ramifications can be frightening. Many people hear, "Move away from everything that's familiar and go to someplace where you know no one, a place I'm not even going to tell you about until you get there," and then stop hearing anything else.[1] The fear of newness can so easily prevent the following of God in covenant, but somehow Abraham skips over this fear, and simply goes where he is told. All of Abraham's travels are at God's request. It is God who instigates this relationship and who controls the terms of their time together.

God maintains the initiative when a covenant is established to formalize the relationship.

> As the sun went down, a deep sleep fell upon Abram, and a deep and terrifying darkness descended upon him. Yahweh said to Abram, "Know with certainty that your offspring shall be aliens in a land that does not belong to them. Others will make them slaves and oppress them for four hundred years. Then I myself will judge the nation that they serve, and afterward they shall come out with great wealth. You yourself will go to your ancestors in prosperity; you shall be buried in a good old age."
> Genesis 15:12–15

This statement of God to Abraham is the subject of the covenant that is sealed in the next few verses. Again, covenant is started by God and exists only under God's own terms. As such, the terms seem hardly favorable for Abraham—he will die quietly while his descendants endure four centuries of mistreatment. But there are positive elements, too, including the people's freedom at the end, as well as the promise of descendants to the still-childless Abraham and Sarah.

Although the terms to the covenant are quite discomforting, they are God's terms that express the relationship God and Abraham have had since the beginning. Abraham is God's servant in the work that God is doing in the world; the covenant formalizes and announces that partnership. In the common work, God sets the agenda and Abraham follows. A covenant is no mere agreement between humans and God; it is a clear

---

[1] The second half of Abraham's call, concerning the blessing, becomes the only portion considered important by certain preachers of our generation who wish to portray God as thinking only of how to bless people, usually in material ways. Such preaching forgets the first part of the verse and stifles the authenticity of the fear that comes in following. This theology of material benefit also disregards the rest of the Abraham story, as well as most of the remainder of the Bible.

statement of God's intentions for the world. Covenant thus carries with it the obligations of the individual to perform the tasks God sets forth. A covenant provides marching orders from a God who has taken the lead in the grand parade. We are handed our parts and soon start learning to play the right tune.

Moses

The covenant God establishes through Moses is of a different nature than the covenant with Abraham. Whereas God's covenant with Abraham centers on one individual and his family, the Mosaic covenant is much broader, including the whole nation of Israel. Also, the covenant is much more specific. Abraham's covenant tells what will happen to his descendants in the centuries to come; Moses' covenant gives lists of things for the people to do.

The covenant delivered by Moses contained the Torah or instruction, often called the Law. The translation "law" is an unfortunate one, since it connotes modern meanings of regulation, restriction, limitation, and punishment. Instead, Torah refers to the more positive concepts of instruction, teaching, and guidance. In the covenant of Torah, God gives to the people instruction about how to live. These are obligations for the people to observe, to be sure, but they are not for the purpose of restriction. Like the one with Abraham, the covenant given by God to the whole people through Moses announces God's intention for the time to come. In this case, the time is at hand. The people are given ethical instructions that should affect their lives immediately. God's vision for life on this planet is proclaimed and the nation of Israel is called in obligation to share, as a whole people, the vocation that God gives them.

Thus it must be emphasized that this ancient covenant covers all aspects of life. God's vision for the world is not limited to ideas about what people should be doing on Sabbath or on Sunday mornings during the worship hour. The covenant involves the whole community and the whole life of each individual within it. It is more than just a set of beliefs, a short list of religious acts to be performed, or a long list of forbidden deeds. The covenant sets out a way of life that is faithful to God's purposes in the whole world. At God's initiative, a plan for all creation is announced in this covenant and all humanity is invited to join in bringing this vision to completion. Even today, when the vision has not yet been fully realized in this all-too-imperfect world, the call is still relevant, and reverberates well through our acts of communion.

New Covenant

The idea of a new covenant is often thought to occur only in the New Testament. In fact, new covenant and New Testament are practically interchangeable terms in many people's minds. However, there is an important tradition of new covenants in the Old Testament. Theologically viewed, these covenants appear as announcements of God's vision for the world, rather than as legalistic sets of rules by which God and humanity relate to each other. The continued efforts of God to work with the human race naturally result in further insights into God's vision for the world.

Jeremiah's New Covenant

The most striking example of a new covenant in the Old Testament is that discussed by the prophet Jeremiah. Jeremiah contains a series of poems and prophecies about newness (Jeremiah 31:21–40). These seven poems are announcements and celebrations of God's new work among humankind, based on fresh expositions of God's vision for the world. Thus, though only the fifth poem directly mentions the new covenant, all the prophecies of newness resonate with the essence of covenant—expressions of God's vision for the world and of humanity's potential partnership with God in bringing the vision to completion.

Since the fifth poem of newness concentrates on the new covenant between God and people, let us begin there.

"Behold! Days are coming," an oracle of Yahweh,
"when I will write with the house of Israel and the house
   of Judah
 a new covenant.
It will not be like the covenant that I wrote with their
   ancestors
on the day I seized them by the hands
to bring them out of the land of Egypt.
For they broke my covenant,
even though I myself had married them,"
an oracle of Yahweh.

"This is the covenant that I will write
with the house of Israel after these days,"
an oracle of Yahweh.
"I will give them my Torah in their midst;
upon their hearts will I inscribe it.
I will be God for them,

they will be people for me.
One will never again teach the other,
either neighbor or relative, saying,
'Know Yahweh!'
For everyone will know me,
from the least to the greatest,"
an oracle of Yahweh.
"For I will forget their sin and their guilt;
I will remember it no longer."

Thus says Yahweh,
who gives the sun as a light for day,
who legislated the moon and the stars as light for the
    night,
who stirs up the sea, so its waves roar,
Yahweh Sabbaoth is this one's name!

"If these statutes fail from before me,"
an oracle of Yahweh,
"the seed of Israel would also cease
from being a nation before me forever."

Jeremiah 31:31-36

The poem falls into four sections, as indicated by the divisions in the translation above. The first announces the new covenant, which comes because the old covenant has been broken. God had shared a vision of the world, but the people had sought their own version of reality and lived according to it, instead of in the light of Yahweh's vision. Even though God had been so close to the people of the ancient covenant as to compare it to marriage, there had still been two separate visions of the way life should be. So God begins to explain once more what the divine vision is, again in the hope that the people will respond. The second section, then, talks about the internalization of the covenantal vision. It will be inscribed on the people's hearts; the people will so deeply share God's vision that there will be no need to instruct or remind each other. The third section offers praise of Yahweh Sabbaoth who brings this wondrous new covenant into being, and the final section illustrates how basic the covenant is to Israel's existence: Without God's covenantal vision, the nation has no life.

The chief difference in this new covenant lies not in its content but in its mode of operation. As compared to the earlier covenants, the new covenant does not necessarily demand new actions, but has placed the instructions so deeply within the people that response in obedience is the only conceivable option. Enforcement is no longer a possible category, as it was when God's vision was expressed in instruction, or Torah. Instead, God's thoughts and the people's thoughts become one. This remarkable wish for the world, expressed in Jeremiah's poem of newness, did not come to pass in the prophet's time, nor did it come to its completion in Jesus. In fact, Jesus also spoke of the internalization of covenant in the Sermon on the Mount (especially Matthew 5:17–48), in which Jesus emphasized that the covenantal arrangements were to last forever, with no portion of the law passing away, but instead being applied to thoughts and intentions as well as actions. Jesus concludes with the injunction, "Therefore, be perfect, just as your heavenly Father is perfect" (Matthew 5:48). Despite the visions of God shared by Jeremiah and by Jesus, humanity still insists on its own thoughts and rejects the vision for the world that God has always seen. This new covenant still awaits us, and God keeps insisting that it truly is possible.

The other poems of newness spell out other details of God's new covenant. These are images that are sometimes shocking in their implications. They depict a God who is so radically free that anything is possible; they are exciting images for those persons with religious imagination. But they are also frightening images for those persons who like life as it is, who are at times happy with the status quo. Since we who are in the church are so often both kinds of people at once, these images can tear at us and affect us deeply.

"Set up for yourselves road markers;
put yourself on the highway,
the road on which you had gone.
Return, O maiden Israel,
return to these your cities!
How long will you waver, O turnable daughter?

For Yahweh creates a new thing in the world:
A female will surround a hero."
Jeremiah 31:21–22

The poems of newness begin with a call to return to Israel. Jeremiah prophesied as Israel was about to be sent into exile; already, the prophet's vision extended to the time when the people could return to their land. Although the desperate military attempts to save the nation were doomed to failure, there would eventually be a restoration in the land. It would not be the heroes who made this happen; instead, the women assume a key role. New covenant means an end to gender rankings and an end to military posturing, instead offering a new restoration to life.

Thus says Yahweh Sabbaoth, God of Israel:
"Again will they say this word
in the land of Judah and in its cities,
when I return the captives:
'May Yahweh bless you,
O righteous home,
O mount of holiness!'
They shall reside in it, in Judah and in all its cities,
    together,
farmhands and those who lead the flocks.
For I will satisfy the lives of the weak,
and all the lives of the weary will I fulfill.
Because of this will I awake;
I will look and my sleep will have been pleasant to me."
Jeremiah 31:23–26

The second poem of newness focuses the attention on life in the land to which the Israelites return. In their newly restored land, persons of all walks of life will be at home. The weak and the weary will receive God's special attention and will have the rest and restoration they so richly deserve. This theme of restoration, so prominent in the traditions about bread discussed above, returns in one of its familiar tones: a special concern for the most needy of society. New covenant means an end to social ranking and division; instead, the most needy will be the most helped.

"Behold! Days are coming," an oracle of Yahweh,
"when I shall sow the house of Israel and the house of
    Judah

with human seed and with animal seed.
Just as I have watched over them
to uproot and to demolish,
to destroy and to annihilate and to bring evil,
thus will I watch over them
to build and to plant,"
an oracle of Yahweh.

Jeremiah 31:27–28

The third poem talks about the new sufficiency that will be
in the land. Where there has been destruction and devastation,
God will preside over new construction. Like the bread that
restores, God's gifts are sufficient and will give what is needed
to those who need it. Building and planting, as opposed to
uprooting, demolishing, destroying, and annihilating, is a recurring
theme of Jeremiah.[2] Where there has been damage by others, God
will remove the sickness, with force if needed, and will begin the
long-awaited healing. Such requires new construction and new
efforts in new ways. The construction should not be considered
only as new homes and office buildings; new social institutions
and new connections between people are certainly just as intended here. Whatever is required to form the right society must
be done. New covenant means positive steps and construction,
rather than denigration and oppression.

In those days, they will never say again:
'The ancestors have eaten sour grapes,
and the teeth of the children become numb.'
But everyone will die for one's own sin;
the person who eats sour grapes will numb that one's
    own teeth.

Jeremiah 31:29–30

This part of the prophet's oracle is harder for us to hear:
"Everyone will die for one's own sin." But listen to what is *not*
being said. People will no longer suffer the effects of other
people's wrongdoing. Victimization will cease. In this radical
vision where God's thoughts are shared equally by all, then

---

[2] Jeremiah 1:10 is the first occurrence of this theme in the
prophet's book. In this first instance, God commissions Jeremiah to
make this announcement the central message of his prophetic ministry.
The possibility of new construction once the dangerous parts of society
have been removed is a key issue for Jeremiah.

there should be no sin at all. Each person's responsibility is emphasized. Such is a difficult vision for moderns to face, since we have too often used our religion to tell us that there is no need for guilt or repentance. Sin is a serious matter and must be faced in utter seriousness. God's desire is for a sinless world and God will keep working in that direction, either with us or without us. New covenant means that responsibility is increased so that sin is faced openly and effectively.

> Thus says Yahweh,
> "If the heavens above are measured
> and the foundations of the earth below explored,
> I will reject all the seed of Israel
> because of all they do,"
> an oracle of Yahweh.
>
> Jeremiah 31:37

This sixth poem of newness offers a threat, but the direction of that threat must be clearly understood. Those who face the possibility of calling forth the divine wrath are those who would measure and who would, having sized things up, attempt to control the sufficiency that God provides. In this sense, the text is like the story of King David who ordered a census taken and was punished for it with a plague (2 Samuel 24).[3] Just like manna, the new covenant is not to be controlled—it is a gift to all, at no price. Many of Jesus' parables operate in the same fashion, by showing that God's gracious presence in the world, like mustard seeds, will grow beyond reason in transforming ways that cannot be controlled or limited by human action. New covenant means that God's gifts are not to be controlled by anyone, but to be given freely to all.

> "Behold days are coming,"
> an oracle of Yahweh,
> "when I will build the city for Yahweh,
> from the Tower of Hananel to the Corner Gate.
> The measuring line will again go out opposite it

---

[3] This story in 2 Samuel, however, is a very difficult one, and has other problems. In this version of the story, it is God who orders David to order the plague, so that God can have a reason to punish David. In the version of the story recorded later in 1 Chronicles 21, it is Satan who orders David to take the census. However, the evil of trying to control the power that God gives is clearly stated in both versions.

from the hill of Gareb
and it will go around toward Goah.
All the valley,
even the corpses and the ashes,
and all the terraces over the brook Qidron,
as far as Horse Gate eastward,
will be holy to Yahweh.
It will not be uprooted nor destroyed again,
for eternity."

Jeremiah 31:38–40

The final poem of newness guarantees that God's vision, once implemented, will stay in place permanently. God's city, in part of the vision repeated in Revelation, is a new creation that lasts forever. Likewise, the relationship that God acquires with the people in that city is a permanent one, not to be changed by the whims of time. New covenant means a vision for all time, for the truly long run, and not just for brief gain or advantage.

Together, these poems combine for a powerful picture of God's new covenant. It unites people into a new community that shares the vision of God and works together to make this vision happen. Differences of gender, class, or position in life are erased; instead, those who most need the care of others receive it in the greatest degree. Control and power cease as helpful construction becomes the common goal. Responsibility increases in importance; sin and victimization are removed. Such are the things of which new covenant is made, and these are to be celebrated through each communion consecration of the new covenant until this vision catches hold of each life in the community.

Blood and Covenant

The church rightly remembers during its communion celebrations the words Jesus said about communion during his Last Supper.

Taking a cup and giving thanks, Jesus gave it to them, saying, "Drink from it, all of you. This is my blood of the covenant, which is poured out for many for the removal of sins."

Matthew 26:27–28[4]

---

[4] Mark 14:24 records the words in shorter fashion: "This is my blood of the covenant, which is poured out for many."

The phrase "my blood of the covenant," applied to the cup of wine, is certainly striking. The connection between the images of body and blood and the elements of bread and wine is clear, but that does not explain why the blood is combined with the idea of covenant. As we have seen above, the idea of covenant is certainly appropriate to Jesus' ministry and to the concepts associated with communion, but why is that here tied to Jesus' blood? The answer lies in the book of Zechariah.

Among the Old Testament's book of the twelve prophets lie many biblical gems that go relatively unnoticed in Christian churches today. Phrases from Amos and Micah may be lodged in our memories, and the story of Jonah is familiar to most, but the others are rarely mentioned at all. This is much to our loss, since these books contain astonishing insights into the nature of faith. Certainly, the authors of the New Testament did not neglect this rich resource, especially in telling the story of Jesus' passion.

Right after the words of institution of communion, Matthew tells us that Jesus quotes from Zechariah 13:7b.

> Then Jesus said to them, "All of you shall desert me this
> night, for it is written,
> > 'I will strike the shepherd,
> > and the sheep of the flock will be scattered.'"
> > > > > > > Matthew 26:31

The Gospels make much use of Zechariah's imagery to describe what happened in Jesus' ministry. By using phrases and ideas from Zechariah and other prophets, the Gospel writers and the early Jewish Christian community could describe what they had experienced and heard in ways that people understood. The strange expression "my blood of the covenant" was one of these phrases, so for the meaning to that enigmatic saying our attention turns to Zechariah.

Zechariah 9:9–17 is a rich passage overflowing with vivid language to explain God's coming salvation. Its poetic imagery can be difficult to understand, but its power makes it so worthwhile. The unit divides into three sections for easier study.

> Rejoice greatly, O daughter Zion!
> > Shout aloud, O daughter Jerusalem!
> Your king is coming to you.
> > A righteous rescuer is he,
> humble and riding upon a donkey,

> upon a colt, the foal of a donkey.
> He will cut off the chariot from Ephraim
> and the horse from Jerusalem;
> and the battle bow shall be cut off,
> and he shall speak peace to the nations.
> His dominion shall be from sea to sea,
> and from the River to the ends of the earth.
>
> Zechariah 9:9–10

This passage begins with a resounding call to rejoicing. God's vision for the world, expressed in covenant, gives explicit reason for joy. God's servant comes to remove the instruments of war from the people and to bring the reign of peace to the whole world. Interestingly, Zechariah insists that the weapons of war will be removed from Israel. Usually in the prophets, the portrayals of eventual peace are after Israel's victory in some large conflagration.[5] Zechariah's vision, however, sees peace implemented through the destruction of Israel's weaponry. In accordance with this strange and appropriate image, the king's victorious entry is one of abject humility, on a colt. Again, such an image was taken up by Matthew to describe Jesus' final entry into Jerusalem.

> When they had approached Jerusalem and reached Bethphage, at the Mount of Olives, then Jesus sent two disciples, saying to them, "Go into the village in front of you, and right away you will find a donkey tied, and a colt with her. Release them and bring them to me. If anyone says anything to you, say, 'The Lord needs them.' He will send them right away." This happened to fulfill what had been spoken through the prophet, saying,
>
> "Speak to the daughter of Zion:
> Your king is coming to you,
> humble, riding on a donkey,
> and on a colt, the foal of a donkey."
>
> Matthew 21:1–5

Jesus, as depicted by Matthew, and the king here described by Zechariah are both figures who bring peace through their humility. As such, they both share a vision of the way the world

---

[5] For examples, see Jeremiah 46—51 and Ezekiel 21; 25—32.

should be; through such small signs as a donkey, they bring that vision into reality. God envisions a new peace, a new salvation of the whole world. Such persons share with God in making this vision happen. More about the new salvation comes in the next section of this prophecy by Zechariah, as the oracle now turns its attention to the people being saved.

> As for you,
> > because of the blood of the covenant with you,
> > I will send out your prisoners
> > > from the waterless pit.
> "Return to your stronghold,
> > > O prisoners of hope,"
> > even today I declare.
> > > > Double will I restore to you.
> For I have bent Judah as my bow;
> > I have made Ephraim its arrow.
> I will awake your children, O Zion,
> > against your children, O Greece,
> > > I will make you like a warrior's sword.
> Yahweh will appear over them;
> > God's arrow will go forth like lightning.
> Lord Yahweh will sound the trumpet
> > and march forth in the whirlwinds of the south.
> Yahweh of hosts will enclose them,
> > and they shall devour and tread down the slingers.
> They shall drink their blood like wine,
> > and be full like a bowl,
> > > drenched like the corners of the altar.
> > > > > Zechariah 9:11–15

The painfully martial imagery of this section cannot be denied. The human fighting is to be replaced by God's own action against the enemy. But the first two verses deserve some independent attention. The cause of God's action is the same reason that Jesus gives for partaking of the cup of communion; in both of these instances, the painfully sacrificial nature of the cup is most evident. In both, it is the cup of other's blood that we drink, and that is only acquired at great price by the activity of God. What is purchased through this expenditure of blood for our benefit is most important: the release of the prisoners from a place of hopelessness, a restoration of their hope and of their livelihood, and a new opportunity to work with God. In Zechariah, the partnership involves following the divine warrior into battle against the enemy; in the communion instigated by Jesus, the partnership with God involves following the divine Son of Peace into the transformation of the world into the reign of peace so clearly represented in Zechariah 9:10. In both images, the new vision and the costly blood of the covenant makes possible new partnership with God, by which humans can share in the realization of that vision.

The Zechariah passage concludes with a remarkable hymn of joy that makes even clearer its ties to our ideas of communion.

> On that day
>   Yahweh their God will rescue them
>   like a flock of God's people.
> Like the jewels of a crown
>   they shall shine on God's land.
> For what goodness and beauty are God's!
> Grain shall make the young men flourish,
>   and new wine the young women.
> Zechariah 9:16–17

This conclusion can only be described as a call to communion. God's new salvation is here presented as the clear result of the blood of the covenant, the cost of the vision of a new world. Salvation comes to those who are possessed and tended by God. This salvation of the world for which we long is a time and place of goodness and beauty. Perhaps best of all is the way in which grain and new wine, the same elements that Jesus took and shared with the disciples and that we take as communion, will make all people grow and strengthen. This kind of communion comes at the climax of God's salvation, but communion also keeps calling us onward to work with God to make this salvation for the world a reality. Communion reminds the church of the past saving events of Jesus, but it must also remind us of the future salvation that still awaits our action. Such is the vision into which new covenant, including the covenant whose blood we recall in communion, calls us forward.

The Covenant of Communion

The New Covenant

Communion is one of a long line of covenants and new covenants in the Bible. As such it shares with all the previous covenants their most important aspects. Of first importance is that God instigates the covenant. Any covenant at all, no matter what the terms, focuses attention on God's sovereignty, which is God's absolute right to operate the world as God sees fit. At times, this means new covenants, new visions about the world may shatter our own expectations and understandings about what life should be.

Communion performs such a shattering. For all who have thought that religious rituals are important to the faith, communion's covenant responds that the only ritual is eating, which is surely a simple enough thing for all. There are no barriers against anyone participating in such a ritual; the table extends freely and must include all, or it is not the table of a Jesus who came for all. To those who think that belief is all that religion requires, the new covenant of communion presents a vision of the way the world can and should be. With that vision comes the invitation and the challenge to work with God in bringing that vision to reality, and so right action becomes essential.

Communion, like the other new covenants, demands that gender and status be removed as barriers. Control must be replaced with care and responsibility. A sense of community must take the place of our sense of self-protection. Hope must be restored to ourselves and to all others. We are all to be saved as God's own flock; our actions should reflect that identity.

God's covenants provide a guide both for action and for thought. These are not to be divided. Communion issues a moral challenge for those who would participate in life under the new covenant. Those who accept the challenge find new ways of relating to God and to others as the divine vision for reality becomes of overarching importance. God's covenantal vision transfixes us and transforms us, beginning and re-beginning so often with the act of communion.

The Ever-New Covenant

God's new covenant truly is always new. The challenge keeps coming to us as often as we need it, in order to spur us on to greater commitment and greater action. God's goal has been so clearly expressed in the visions and new covenants God has given us over the many years, and that goal is a whole and saved world. The means of accomplishing this goal is the partnership that God desires with all humanity. At times, there is blood with these new covenants, because the work of transforming the world is a costly one. The release of those imprisoned and the realization of hope for all is an extremely expensive operation. Nevertheless, the message of Abraham, of Moses, of Jeremiah, and of Jesus, each the recipient and the transmitter of a new vision and a new covenant, is that God will stop at nothing to save the world. Time and time again, we humans must stop and stare in amazement at what this means. God will stop at nothing to save the world! Through visionary covenants, God invites us to join in saving the world, which means sharing the joys and the costs with the One who was rejoicing in humanity at the very moment of creation and also with the One who has been experiencing the pain and the cost in ways greater than we can imagine. The covenant of communion calls us to this sharing; the invitation to the table asks us to join in and to accept the task.

9

---

atoning sacrifice

If someone wants to discover our culture, to understand who we are as a people and see what makes us tick inside, the best place to go is to the movies. Motion pictures have been one of the most enduring and pervasive elements of our popular culture through the majority of this century. There are "summer" movies, usually of the action-adventure variety, that start in late spring and go through the start of school in the fall. For Americans, summer is the time to be outside, and the summer movies are full of outdoor things. By the end of summer, when it gets too hot to go outside, the movie theaters offer more comedies, so we can take a short escape from the world even if we can't afford the vacation that provides the escape we really want. Christmas movies are more typically tearjerkers; commercially packaged sentimentality is, after all, the theme of the American Christmas. In between summer and Christmas are the fall movies. They are the serious ones for adults, because fall is the time of school and education, the right time for being sophisticated and adult. Whatever the time of year, movies reflect what most people are feeling or want to feel.

Of all the movies of the last decade, one receives the most discussion in Old Testament classes. In *Raiders of the Lost Ark*, a colorful, swashbuckling archaeologist named Indiana Jones ventures throughout the world in search of buried antiquities. His interests are only scientific, but he is surrounded by selfish, power-hungry manipulators. In this movie, Indiana Jones goes to find the ark of the covenant, the biblical box from Moses' time that had been used by Israel's armies. When the ark went before the army into battle, victory was certain. At least, that was what the Israelites thought; several Old Testament stories provide the exceptions.[1] Unscrupulous persons of all sorts are chasing after the buried ark in Indy's time, and so he chases it, too, in order to get there first. The climax of the story comes when the villains have gained control of the ark and decide to open it, while our heroes wait nearby. In marvelous special effects, spirits and powers pour out of the opened ark, devouring those who raided the lost ark, but preserving Indiana Jones and the heroine.

For persons of faith, the strange and surreal scene is easy to understand. Those who violate God's sacredness pay the painful price for their transgression, but the heroes gain salvation from their enemies by God's power. God's box is full of powerful energies waiting to be unleashed, and the wrongdoing of the villains let that awesome power out of the box. Once free, God's power shoots through the sky, and though it seems uncontrolled, God's activity is not random. Because the villains are destroyed by God, the heroes go free, their salvation purchased by the deserved death of their opponents.

When I think about the thrilling end to *Raiders of the Lost Ark*, I am reminded of the emphasis on atonement that is often expressed in communion. Although these ideas make a good movie, I wonder if they are appropriate ideas for our theological reflection around communion. I remember hearing communion meditations that come close to a theology of Indiana Jones: God is powerful and often angry because there is sin and wrongdoing in the world, and God once unleashed that awful angry force. Fortunately for us, though, the full impact of God's anger fell on Jesus, and so we were saved from that anger. The difference between *Raiders of the Lost Ark* and Christianity is straightforward: The God of Indiana Jones and the ark destroys the guilty party, but the God of Jesus Christ strikes and kills the innocent savior, who saves because the bolts of God's anger miss us to hit him, even though we are the guilty ones.

In theological terms, this view of God is called substitutionary atonement. According to this view, all people are guilty sinners, destined for death and destruction because of that sin. Jesus Christ is pure, the only sinless one in earth's history.

---

[1] See especially 1 Samuel 4—6.

Although it is God's nature to hate sin, it is also God's nature to love people. God intends to destroy people because of their sin, but God thinks up a way to save people from God's own deathly anger. If there was one perfect person, God could destroy that sinless one instead of all the sinners. The only remaining problem was that no sinless people were available, so God incarnated the divine self into the human Jesus (who was both completely human and completely divine). The miracle of the cross, then, was that God in the form of Jesus volunteered to receive God's punishment of death. On the cross, God kills God, and God's anger depletes itself. Of course, since God cannot be killed, God raises God back to life. Afterward, there is no more anger and the penalty of death is never enforced again on those who truly deserve it. Jesus has substituted himself for sinners in accepting the death penalty. It was as if a lightning rod was placed near Indiana Jones' ark right before it was opened, and the lightning rod absorbed all the divine power before it could hurt anyone, sucking God's power into the ground where no one ever saw it again and where everyone on earth would be safe (or saved) from it.

Despite the appeal of the notion of substitutionary atonement, its problems are many. It depicts a violent, bloodthirsty God that seems antithetical to the God of whom Jesus speaks. God's mercy becomes equated with the fundamental injustice that the guilty go free and an innocent one is punished. Such doctrine virtually denies any true notion of God's justice. Furthermore, it places all of God's saving activity in the past, with little need if any for a church of God's followers who are working out their salvation with utter seriousness (Philippians 2:12–13).

These ideas of atonement have become a pervasive element of our communion language. Our table-talk refers to Christ's sacrificial and atoning death for the forgiveness of our sins. However, we rarely pause to reflect on Old Testament ideas of sacrifice and atonement. Since the New Testament understands salvation and Jesus' death in terms often taken from Old Testament thoughts, one must investigate the Old Testament's ways of thinking about sacrifice and atonement in order to comprehend communion.

Sacrifice in Ancient Israel

Ancient Israel's religion observed several types of sacrifices. In all of their many forms, sacrifices served to worship God.

Although ancient Israel knew their God did not need food to eat, the sacrifices still honored God and asserted that God did rule their lives. Sacrifice was an act of personal devotion between a worshiper and God; it created a special, personal bond and reinforced it throughout the years as the offerings continued. Likewise, sacrifice was a public statement, affirming the faith of the whole community.

All ritual acts of religion share these basic characteristics. As an example, consider modern understandings of baptism. This is a special act that creates a bond between the baptized and God; this bond grows throughout the years from a one-time act of devotion to a lifelong relationship of commitment. Baptism is also a public act; it empowers the whole community to observe such a powerful assertion that Jesus is Lord. The church performs baptisms for the same reason that ancient Israel performed sacrifices: God commands these acts and God's people, while following in obedience, deepen their relationship to God, as individuals and as a community of faith. In these acts of worship, faith deepens.

Of the several different types of sacrifice recorded in the Old Testament, those most often mentioned are the whole burnt offerings. Bulls, goats, sheep, and birds could be burnt offerings. In each case, the priest cut the animal into pieces and placed all the pieces upon the altar, where fire consumed the animal (Leviticus 1). Burnt offerings celebrated God's presence among the people; the smoke rising from burning animal symbolized the connection between earth and God's heaven. Holy days always included burnt offerings as reminders of the God whom the Israelites served (Leviticus 23). These sacrifices were performed as a regular part of the temple service. Rather than expressing God's presence with any individual, offering sacrifices was a corporate activity, under the responsibility of the priests. Burnt offerings were a central part of the worship of God.

Grain offerings often accompanied the burnt offerings. The person offering a burnt offering would also bring a small amount of grain, probably baked into loaves of bread, to give to the priest (Numbers 15:1–10). The priests of the temple and their families would eat this bread (Leviticus 6:14–18; 7:8–10). Another kind of bread was the bread placed on the altar, where it would sit for a week in order to be filled with the smoke from the burnt offerings. Thus imbued with God's holy presence, the priests would eat the smoky, stale bread in order to partake of the presence (Exodus 35:13). Also, the worshiper would bring a drink offering of wine, so that the priests would have something to drink along with their bread. These additions to the burnt offering allowed the priests to eat and to join in the celebration marked by the worshiper's offering of the animal. Often an offering of incense would add a festive ambience or a sense of sacredness to the sacrifice (Exodus 30; Numbers 16).

A special category of sacrifice, called the peace offering, expressed the community's joy in celebrating God's goodness. Never a required offering, it was an additional act of worship to express special thankfulness. The whole community shared these peace offerings, with a special portion belonging to the priests as their due (Exodus 29:26–28). Any special blessing felt by an Israelite would be the occasion for a peace offering, usually of a ram. Meat was expensive in these ancient times, so any meal with meat was a rarity. Peace offerings provided a means for persons to celebrate their bounty before God, with established ways to help the priests and to share the food with others. During a peace offering, the entire animal would have to be eaten in a short span of time (Leviticus 19:5–8), so other people would be invited to share the feast. Family and friends might be first on the list, but food would still be left over. In a culture without refrigerators or other techniques for preserving food, the slaughtered animal would require a large number of people to eat it. Perhaps the needy would be invited so that they would be able to eat. Peace offerings mean both celebration and sharing.

The Sin Offering

When modern Christians think of ancient Israel's sacrificial system, perhaps the most frequently remembered type of sacrifice is the sin offering. In many respects, sin offerings seem just like the other offerings mentioned above. They involved the priest's slaughter of an animal brought by a worshiper. The rationale behind the sin offering, though, differed radically from the ideas represented by other offerings. Burnt offerings expressed God's presence in all forms of worship, peace offerings gave cause for celebration throughout the community, and grain and drink offerings provided food for priests, whereas the sin offering more directly affected the relationship between the worshiper and God.

Sin offerings facilitated forgiveness. When someone had sinned by violating God's instructions, a sacrifice of an animal allowed the restoration of a right relationship. Unlike the case with the peace offering, the sinner did not eat from the sin offering; instead, it became part of the priests' due (Leviticus 5:12, 16; 7:6–10). The type of animal to be sacrificed depended upon the financial capabilities of the sinner. Although a bull, lamb, or goat was often sacrificed, other acceptable offerings included pigeons or just a small bit of flour (Leviticus 4:1—6:7; Numbers 15:22–31). This is important: The offering required a commitment on the part of the sinner and thus had to be a significant item, but it was not designed to be punitive. God's law never places unreasonable demands upon the sinner, but it does require the acceptance of proper responsibility. For these and other reasons, simplistic interpretations of the sin offering must be avoided; this is hardly a transaction where an animal's death is traded for the salvation of a human soul.

Several other elements combind to make the sin offering effective. Firstly, the sinner recognized the sin, perhaps through seeing the negative effects of that sin. Only after recognition did the sinner begin the process of seeking forgiveness. Secondly, restitution was given: When someone commited a wrong against another person, the sinner had to restore what had been lost. The Old Testament law required that the loss be paid in full, plus 20 percent more (Leviticus 6:5). The human suffering caused by human sin received due attention; there was no forgiveness until the results of one's sin had been treated and made right. Thirdly, a confession was made (Leviticus 5:5). The problem received a public statement, which served both as an instruction to others and as an affirmation of faith's power to restore relationships between God and persons. Lastly, the sin offering was publicly sacrificed. The process of sin's removal ended here in the public worship of God.[2]

Note that God's anger was not a factor in the sin offering. In fact, there is no indication at all that God had been angered by the sinner. Instead, God provided a way for sin to be removed from human situations. This plan for the removal of the sin involves realization, commitment, restitution, confession, and worship, but not anger. To the contrary, ancient Israel repeat-

---

[2] Perhaps baptism should be understood in the same way. John's baptism involved repentance, followed by confession and resulting in baptism as an act of public worship affirming the removal of sin (Mark 1:4–5).

edly affirmed that God's greatest gift to them was the Torah. These instructions did not demonstrate divine wrath; they proved God's love by providing and illuminating safe paths in which the people could walk.

In this context, it becomes difficult to talk about "forgiveness." Our modern use of language has severely limited that word. To us, "I forgive you" often means "I'll stop being mad at you." Likewise, "I'm sorry" means "I wouldn't have done what I did if I had known you'd be so mad at me about it. Please stop being mad at me." Thoughts like this are far apart from the ways that God works to remove sin. In the Old Testament, emotions such as feeling sorry and being mad do not appear at all. Instead, the emphasis is on the right actions: removing the effects of sin from those who were victimized and worshiping God in public through offerings. Such acts, according to ancient Israel's understandings, restored not only relationships among humans, but also the relationship between God and the sinner. Without these actions of restoration, the effects of sin would continue to ravage the sinner as well as the rest of the community.

Communion and Sacrifice

The church has often understood communion as similar to the sacrifices of the Old Testament. Many communion meditations explain that in the days of the Old Testament, the Jews sacrificed animals in order to purchase temporary forgiveness, but in the New Testament, Jesus came and offered himself as a sacrifice for our sins, once and for all, so that now there need be no more sacrifices of animals, because Jesus purchased our permanent forgiveness with his own blood. Although such theological statements do contain certain notions of truth, they do not reflect the sacrificial system of ancient Israel as the Old Testament records it.

The Christian sacrament of communion shares certain similarities with Old Testament sacrifices. Communion is a shared meal in response to God's overwhelming goodness. Thus, it is similar to the peace offerings, in that it celebrates the joy of God's benefits through the sharing of a meal. Such aspects of celebration are discussed above in chapter 5. Similarly, chapter 3 presents some similarities between communion and the bread offerings, which fills with God's presence through its time on the altar and then symbolizes God's indwelling of the people through the partaking of the bread.

Communion shares certain themes and patterns with peace offerings and bread offerings, but does not correspond exactly to either of them. Communion is a fundamentally new experience, not a recasting of any of Israel's older traditions.

However, there are great differences between communion and the sin offering, which is the only sacrifice that confronts sin. One of the most noticeable marks of the sin offering is that the guilty worshipers do not partake of the offered food. On the other hand, all of the people partake of communion. Also, communion is a sharing of bread and wine, not a sacrifice of meat. The Passover meal included roast lamb as well as bread and wine; there was no reason that Jesus' last supper could not have focused on the meat. Events were different than that, however, and the church recorded almost nothing about the meat at that meal; the meat was not the significant event. Communion does not follow the tradition of the ancient Israelite sin offering; the forgiveness of sin is *not* the intended result of participation in communion.

Close attention to Jesus' words over the cup can result in a better understanding of the meaning of communion. Three of the Gospels relate the events of a Passover meal during the week of Jesus' passion, but neither Mark 14:22–26 or Luke 22:14–23 connect Jesus' last supper to the forgiveness of sins. Matthew's version of the last supper contains an important difference from these other Gospel accounts.

> Taking a cup and giving thanks, Jesus gave it to them, saying, "Drink from it, all of you. This is my blood of the covenant, which is poured out for many for the removal of sins."
>
> Matthew 26:27–28

Matthew's point is clear: The cup of communion represents Jesus' blood. The important difference does not stop there though. Jesus' poured-out blood serves as a metaphor for Jesus' death, and his death affects sins. Death and blood enter us into God's covenant, where surprising and unpredictable things happen. Relationship with God and entry into the realm of covenant, where God acts most seriously, brings God's everlasting concerns to bear. God always works to remove sin, and especially so in the death of Jesus.

This passage from Matthew connects Jesus' death to the communion practices that memorialize both Jesus' death and life. Jesus' death has the power to remove sin. Communion celebrates that power, but the church's practice of communion must go further than that. Jesus' death and resurrection are more than the expression of divine power; they are assertions in faith of the direction that power takes. God is effective against sin; the removal of sin actually takes place. For this reason, the community joins in communion, as part of the worship of the God who removes sin.

This understanding of communion parallels the function of the Old Testament's sin offering. Restitution removed the effects of sin by restoring the losses of those who had suffered as a result of the sin. Through the restoration and the confession, sinners confronted the problems that their sins had caused, and their actions, through God's grace, solved those problems.[3] Then, worship concluded the removal of sin.

Likewise, through Jesus sin—our sin and the sin of the world—is removed; communion is that part of worship that celebrates sin's prior removal. Communion does not cause sins to be forgiven; it is not a sacrament that brings a magic cleansing to the believer. Instead, communion remembers and celebrates Jesus' blood, which was poured out for the forgiveness of sin. In communion, the community worships God, who constantly reminds us of the need to avoid and remove sin.

Communion is not a repeated sacrifice that brings forgiveness. It is what the people do *because* of sin's removal. There is no magic in the bread and wine that washes away sin and guilt, but there is a God of whom the bread and wine remind us, and that God works constantly to rid the world of sin. Through God, we are free from sin.

Atonement

The concept of atonement has been a difficult one for the church. Like the other theological notions of sacrifice, atonement is rooted in ancient practices of the Israelite temple, and those ancient practices seem very foreign to us. Nevertheless, much of the talk around the communion table centers on atonement as a way of understanding what the bread and the wine recall. The church usually presents atonement in much the

------

[3] Walter Brueggemann, *Finally Comes the Poet: Daring Speech for Proclamation* (Minneapolis: Fortress Press, 1989), pp. 23–33.

same way that it understands sacrifices for sin: Atonement is an act with divine consequences that removes God's anger from the people. However, atonement takes a much different form in the Old Testament.

In the Old Testament understanding, atonement takes place in two ways. Normally, atonement is the result of the sin offerings, but Yom Kippur, the Day of Atonement, is also a special atonement. When the legal texts discuss the sin offerings, atonement is the goal of the worship. The priest makes atonement for the people through the sacrifice of an animal, and the people then receive forgiveness.[4] The condition of atonement refers to the act of worship that concludes and confirms the whole process of removal of sin. Atonement is not the removal of sin, but the *celebration* of sin's removal.

The Day of Atonement, Yom Kippur, is one of the most holy days within the ancient Israelite and the modern Jewish calendars.[5] On that day and on no other day throughout the year, the high priest enters into the innermost part of the temple, the Holy of Holies. The high priest must wear special clothes and must make a special sin offering for himself and for his family, in order to cleanse himself for this very important task. A goat is also offered as a special sin offering with a different purpose. In all the other atonements, the priest makes atonement for people, but here the priest makes atonement for places—first, the holy place of the sanctuary, and then the altar itself (Leviticus 16:16, 18). Then the high priest can again offer burnt offerings in worship of God, to bring the atonement to the people who celebrate sin's removal (Leviticus 16:24).

What does it mean to make atonement for a place? This is obviously a very different understanding of atonement than what modern churches normally present. The Day of Atonement functions differently than the other sacrifices that provide atonement for individuals by removing their sins. Instead, the Day of Atonement cleanses a holy place so that the place can continue functioning in worship, especially in its role of removing the sins of people. In ancient Israel the temples and their altars were where forgiveness began. If the temple was sinful, then there could be no

---

[4]For biblical references, see Leviticus 4:20, 26, 31, 35; 5:6, 10, 13, 16, 18; 6:7, 30.

[5]See chapter 4, p. 64, for one of the rabbinical stories related to Yom Kippur. The biblical instructions for the Day of Atonement can be found in Leviticus 16.

forgiveness from sin for anyone. Only when the temple and the priests were pure could sin receive effective treatment. Temples could become unclean in many ways, from the abomination of offering detestable offerings upon the altar to the sin of the priests. More than that, the temple's purity was daily threatened by the throngs of people who made their offerings there. The sins of the whole people confronted the temple on a regular basis. The Day of Atonement was important because it provided a way to cleanse the temple and the priests. Without such a special, annual atonement, the forgiveness for others would not have worked as it was intended to function in the removal of sins.

The Old Testament records a complex system of sacrifices, including the Day of Atonement. During the period of the Israelite monarchy, the temple priests were probably in the process of developing this system in its current form. They would have participated in worship similar to this, but all the rules and exceptions were not yet in place. After Babylon conquered the Israelites and took them into exile for two or three generations, a group of Jews emigrated to Jerusalem and constructed there another temple on the ruins of the former one. This new temple stood for almost six hundred years. In this second temple, the full set of rules and regulations may have reached their official status. By the time of Jesus, this sacrificial system had been standard for five centuries, reflecting an even longer history. For many early Christians, it was still expected that they would continue to participate in the sacrifices of the temple, since such sacrifices were vital elements of the Jewish religion to which Jesus had adhered.

An all-important change in the Christian religion came about forty years after Jesus, in the year 70, when a military invasion destroyed the second temple. To this date, the temple has not been reconstructed. Without the temple, the sacrificial system suddenly stopped. The old ways of worshiping God could no longer be performed. Both Judaism and Christianity needed to find new ways of expressing their faith. Perhaps each group's different solutions to this problem caused the rift between Judaism and Christianity. This rift continues to this day, in large part because of Christianity's attacks on Judaism.[6] Although

---

[6] For a clear discussion of Jewish-Christian relations, see Walter Harrelson and Randall M. Falk, *Jews and Christians: A Troubled Family* (Nashville: Abingdon Press, 1990).

both groups chose nonsacrificial means of religion, the other differences grew greater. For Christians, the lack of a temple broke the final tie with Jewish faith, and documents such as the Letter to the Hebrews became more important.[7]

Hebrews contains an intricate argument about the relationship between Judaism and Christianity. In the view of the author of this letter, the sacrificial system of the temple, with nearly a millennium of tradition behind it, provides a way of understanding Jesus. Although this letter argues the superiority of Jesus over the old system, it also presents a view of Jesus that would be absolutely meaningless without a faith in the temple. One of the great problems for modern Christians in understanding the Letter to the Hebrews is that it assumes knowledge of the temple and a deep belief in the saving effects of the sacrifices in the temple and other events. On the basis of such a belief, Hebrews shows that Jesus acts in ways that are very similar to and better than the temple and its priests. The idea of atonement appears in closest connection to Jesus in Hebrews 9 and 10.

> Christ entered once for all into the Holy Place, not through the blood of goats and calves, but through his own blood, thus obtaining eternal redemption. For if the blood of goats and bulls and the sprinkling of a heifer's ashes makes holy those who have been made unclean, so that their flesh is cleansed, how much more will the blood of Christ, who through the eternal Spirit offered himself without blemish to God, cleanse our conscience from dead works to worship the living God!
>
> Hebrew 9:12–14

The author's argument here can be difficult to follow, but a grounding in Old Testament sacrificial law proves most helpful. Although atonement is not mentioned explicitly, it is certainly what lies behind the thoughts of this text.[8] Here again is the same

---

[7] Most scholars agree that the book of Hebrews was written before the destruction of the second temple. However, the continuance of its use may well have been guaranteed by the destruction of the temple, since this book provides alternative ways of acting out the Christian faith without a temple.

[8] The connection is made explicit in Hebrews 9:25, where the reference to an annual sacrifice in the Holy Place appears. Within the ancient Israelite sacrificial system, this could only refer to the Day of Atonement.

understanding of atoning sacrifices as found in Leviticus: The sacrifice is the act of worship that *follows* salvation and the removal of sin. However, what Christ has done is different from the continuing sacrifices of ancient Israel. Christ's actions are unique.

> Christ has now appeared once, until the completion of the age, for the nullification of sin through his own sacrifice.
> Hebrews 9:26b

Although Christ leads the usual worship that results from sin's removal, something more is done. Christ nullifies sin. When sin is removed, it can return, as it always had done throughout history; but when sin is nullified, it is permanently removed.[9] What has been nullified cannot return. Because of Jesus, the freedom from sin is permanent. This is a remarkably strong statement that runs against so much of human experience: Because of Jesus' death, there can be no sin. In the view of such a statement, people can no longer commit wrong acts. Evil's effects are still present in the world, however. The complete absence of evil is a vision for which we all long. We eagerly await Jesus because our salvation is not yet complete. There is still evil and we still feel its effects; we even still join in the evil acts that surround us. The nullification of sin has not yet happened, though it is the intended result of Jesus' sacrifice.[10] The life and death of Jesus move toward the nullification of sin and make that nullification inevitable, though there is still another step in the process.

----

[9] In Greek, the term for removal is *aphesis*, usually translated as "forgiveness." It is a common term used through the New Testament, corresponding to the Hebrew word *nasa'*, which means "to lift up." Sins that are "forgiven" or "removed" are lifted away from the sinner, thus having no more effect, unless the sins return. The term for nullification is the much stronger word *athetesis*, usually rendered "removal." Nullification seems to end the possibility of sin's return.

[10] Note also Hebrews 10:1, where the author states that the annual sacrifices do not create perfection within the worshipers. Of course, the ancient sacrificial system never claimed to bring perfection, but only to provide cleanness and to celebrate the sins that had already been removed through restitution and confession. Perfection of Christians must be the goal of Jesus' activity, according to the author of Hebrews. Jesus does for the worshipers what the old sacrifices could never do; Jesus can lead people to perfection. This understanding, though troublesome in the modern church, reminds one of other New Testament statements, such as Matthew 5:48, that insist on perfection as the only proper goal for believers.

This chapter from Hebrews, then, cannot be discussing a present condition where sin is absent from the world. Although Christ's actions have been once and for all, sin still exists in the world. In fact, the author of the Letter to the Hebrews must have been trying to solve this problem. Why is there still sin in the world if Jesus' mission on earth was to do something about sin? Did Jesus fail? Must we go back to the sacrifices of the temple as the *only* way to remove sin? The author of this letter insists on the importance and effectiveness of Jesus' earthly activity. Christ must have performed that once-for-all action for some other reason than the removal of sin. The key lies in the next chapter:

> By God's will, we have been sanctified through the offering of the body of Jesus Christ once for all.
>
> Hebrews 10:10

Christ came not to assure people that God is not mad at them for being sinners; that popular interpretation misses the point of this passage altogether. Likewise, Christ did not come merely to take away past sins from those who believe. The real intent goes much, much further. Jesus' goal is the sanctification of all people. To sanctify is to make holy, just as the Holy Place of the old temple was made holy each year through the Day of Atonement.[11] Thus, what Christ came to do was to make people holy, just as the temple was made holy; both times this is called atonement.

Jesus' atonement sanctifies the people. What does this mean though? The atonement of the ancient temple purified it for a reason: so others' sins could be effectively removed. Through a properly operating temple that was truly holy and sanctified, the removal of sin was made possible far beyond the boundaries of the temple itself; atonement assured the continued operation of the temple. Atonement enables sin's removal. Too often, the church today confuses atonement and the removal of sin, but these are distinct ideas. Jesus came not to remove sin, but to atone for the sins of all the people, thus enabling the removal of sin to continue far beyond the boundaries of those whom Jesus directly touched. In such an under-

---

[11] The Greek word here, *egiasmenoi,* "sanctified, made holy," is related to the word *agios,* "consecrated, holy." Thus, it connects to the Holy Place, where atonement takes place, whether it is the atonement of ancient Israelite sacrifices or of Jesus' once-for-all sacrifice.

standing the church today can comprehend and claim such statements as Jesus' promise to Peter and to the whole church: "Whatever you bind on earth will be bound in heaven, and whatever you release on earth will be released in heaven" (Matthew 16:19;18:18). The keys to heaven are ours, not so that we can let ourselves in more easily, but so that we can help others to enter heaven. The Letter to the Hebrews continues by discussing this entry into the holy places of the sanctuary and heaven.

> My brothers and sisters, we have confidence to enter the Holy Place through the blood of Jesus, who dedicated for us a new and alive way through the curtain, which is his flesh. We also have a great priest over the house of God. Therefore, let us approach with a true heart in fullness of faith, having our hearts sprinkled clean from an evil conscience and having our bodies washed with pure water. Let us hold tightly the confession of our unwavering hope, because the one who has promised is faithful. Let us consider how to arouse each other for love and good deeds, not forsaking the common assemblies, as some make a habit. Instead, let us encourage each other, even more as you see the Day approaching. If we sin voluntarily after having received the knowledge of the truth, there no longer remains a sacrifice for sins, but a fearful prospect of judgment, and a fire of fury to consume those who intend to oppose.
>
> Hebrews 10:19–27

We are sanctified once-for-all through Jesus' atoning sacrifice, and once we are sanctified, we are enabled to remove the sins of others. Thus we can—and must—be busy at the task of urging each other to love and to good works (Hebrews 10:24). Once sanctified, the perfection of ourselves and of the world becomes our goal, just as the worldwide removal of sin and its effects is the goal of God.

Communion's Atoning Sacrifice

This atoning sacrifice of Jesus becomes the subject for our remembering at communion. We ponder the bread, we peer deeply into the cup, and we think about that sacrifice. As we reflect, we reminisce about the atonement that purifies and sanctifies us, and we also think about the task with which Jesus left us. As we partake of communion, we join the community of Jesus' priests, the priesthood of all believers, who continue to remove sin from the world. We watch our own lives to reduce and end the sin that we find there. We work with others to heal and to restore, in order to deal effectively with the world's sin. As Christ's priests, we bring forgiveness to the world and we work to transform the world in order to remove its sin. As always, the key elements are restitution that leads to justice, confession that reinvigorates the community, and worship that reminds of the sacrifice. For us, communion must be part of that worship.

Communion is not a once-for-all act, lodged in the distant past. Communion is not merely something that causes us to remember what happened long ago. Communion is a present activity for God's people that expresses and renews commitment, a commitment to a new kind of life with God. Atonement is much the same. Atonement cleanses us so that we can work with God in the healing of the whole world, in the here and now. Communion and atonement transcend the past acts of Jesus and enter firmly into the present life of the church. A church in communion is a church that is constantly in the midst of atonement, and this experience begins the healing of the world.

Communion brings hope in the face of sin. Although the deeds of the world surround us and at times depress us, the church is no place for us to hide from that sin. Instead, around Christ's table, we commit ourselves to that ancient task: the removal of sin. Communion challenges us to a task that may seem impossible, but communion also empowers us. We have good reason to hope, because of what Christ has done for us through that long-ago and still-current atoning sacrifice. Challenge and hope combine with purity of sight and clarity of purpose. God intends a world without sin, and God's partners enter into covenant to undertake that task when we gather at the communion table.

10

death and life

One of the most ominous words in the English language is "fate." To many ears, it sounds just like "doom"—the unavoidable evil that lurks in the future. Some persons of theological affinity will interpret fate in potentially positive contexts, such as predestination for salvation or the friendly presence of a loving God at the gates of heaven, but mostly fate is a scary thing.

Our language can hardly contain our preoccupation with fate. We have innumerable cliches and sayings about fate or, as it is called by those who prefer longer words, inevitability. One's future can be written in stone, or one can read the writing on the wall (both are Old Testament images). Sometimes one's fate is fixed in the stars. The future can be as sure as can be, or it can be sure as shootin'. Often, though, our language goes in the other direction: fate is not fixed and there is no complete certainty. One can never be too careful. Nothing lasts forever. Of all the ways to talk about inevitability or the lack thereof, one expression tells it all: There's nothing certain except death and taxes.

It's possible to be skeptical about that, though. Taxes may seem inevitable, but so many people seem able to avoid them. Some of the richest people will even say that taxes are just for the "little people." How we wish we could deny this! However, in too many instances the rich have seemed to walk away from their responsibilities without anyone to stop them, while the poor are too often held to higher standards by those who enforce such things.

Even if we wish not to ponder such things, it seems obvious to everyone that avoiding death and taxes is big business. We may think they are inevitable, but we'll do anything we can to avoid them, or at least postpone them. Tax advisers, C.P.A.s, tax lawyers, and financial consultants, all help people minimize their exposure to taxation. Medical doctors, in all their various specialties, develop ever more ways to care for the critically ill, from high-tech intensive care units filled with multi-million dollar machines to home care and hospices to provide the human touch. Each year, financial services and health care grow into larger portions of our nation's expenditures. The attempt to escape death and taxes may be doomed to failure, but that doesn't seem to stop anyone from trying.

Even when we say that nothing's inevitable except death and taxes, death truly grabs our attention. Taxes may be unavoidable, but death is *final*. Because it is so final, death is the greater moral question of our age. We may ruin the careers of politicians who cheat on their taxes (or we may reelect them with impunity, as happens too often), but we each face the myriad questions of modern medical ethics, from contraception, abortion, and infant mortality rates to suicide, euthanasia, and the rising costs of health care.

As Christians, the Bible sometimes frustrates us by saying so little that fits directly these highly nuanced questions of the modern debates. Perhaps that is because our medical issues concentrate on health and quality of life, as we accept the inevitability of death and try to shore up our defenses against it as strongly as we can, knowing that in the end each defense loses to death's offensive onslaught. Many texts of the Bible, however, refuse to surrender and make the amazingly incredible claim: not even death is truly inevitable.

This claim cuts against all of our experience and yet it voices all of our hope. The idea that some persons can escape death seems completely unrealistic to us; the Bible's stories of resurrections are too miraculous for belief. Nevertheless, they express a central theological truth: God undergirds the universe in such a way that even death is subject to God. This miraculous nature of God finds its expression when Elijah raises the widow's son, when Jesus performs a similar wonder, when Lazarus walks forth from the cavern of the dead, and when Paul raises a sleepy listener.

The Bible claims that death is not inevitable, but in other places it makes one other claim that actually embraces our apprehensive experiences and voices all of our deepest fears. There are times when death, whether inevitable or not, should not be avoided. Only the acceptance of death allows the greater meaning to be understood. Through suffering and even through death, the true message of God goes forth. The beheading of John the Baptist, the martyrdom of Stephen, and the crucifixion of Jesus are deaths that bring meaning to the absurdity of mortality.

Communion celebrates and mourns both death and life. Jesus' last meal marks death but also remembers life. Deep within communion, one finds death and life mingled, and God throughout it all.

Elijah and the Widow's Son

In chapter 3, we watched as the prophet Elijah met a widow (1 Kings 17). This widow befriended Elijah and fed him at his request, even though she and her son were at the brink of death from starvation, because she was so poor. Through hospitality, the bread multiplied until there was enough for everyone. There was provision for Elijah, and the woman and her son ate and lived. God's bountiful, sufficient bread brought life and salvation to them, through faith and hospitality. But the story does not end there.

> After these things, the son of the woman who ruled the house became ill. His illness was so severe that no breath remained in him. She then said to Elijah, "What have you against me, O man of God? You have come to me to make me remember my sin and to kill my son!" Then he said to her, "Give me your son."
>
> 1 Kings 17:17–19a

Faith brought bread, and bread brought life, but would this life only bring death? Death is inevitable, we would say. Life eventually leads to death. Even if death is delayed for a while, its inexorable approach continues. Of course, the son dies. Everyone dies. Death is inevitable. The woman watches in pain as the very breath ebbs out of her only son, leaving her utterly alone in a world of cruelty and pain. Faced with meaningless death, life is chaos, formless and void. From the midst of this chaos, she cries out against Elijah, who had once brought life but now seemed empty-handed. "Why do you hate me, Elijah?"

she cries. "If you have the power of life and death, why do you choose death for my son?" Why would death ever be chosen?

The widow knows one other thing, something too dark to speak: death spreads. When she was left with no husband, her society considered her among the lowest of all persons. Food would be scarce and recognition would be impossible. But at least she had a son, and that son could help with things. The son, if he did nothing else, promised a future of care and provision. She could raise her little boy as a loving son who would honor his mother and care for her when she was unable to protect herself. But if the son dies, then what will be left for the widow? When she holds the corpse in her arms, she must mourn the death of her future as well.

But the widow's musings take other dark paths as well. She wonders if her son's death resulted from her own sin. Has her sin festered until it has rotted into death that first infected her husband and now her son? Is repeated death to be her punishment for sins that are as yet unlisted? The horrible questions surge through her mind in a flash flood of fear, threatening to drown out her very self.

Elijah's demand is unexpected and stark. Staring into her pain-filled eyes as the anger of her well-justified shouting echoes from the walls, his still, small voice comes through: "Give me your son." How would the widow have reacted? The corpse was all she had left, and now this prophet wished to take that away too. Then she would be completely alone, without even a body over which to grieve.

If she would have had time to think, her mind could have wandered through the ancient stories and lighted on another tale of horror and woe, when God commanded Abraham to sacrifice Isaac, his only son (Genesis 22). He took his son up a tall mountain, placed the boy on the wood that Isaac had carried up the trail, tied him firmly to that funeral pyre, raised the knife into the air, and aimed squarely at the heart of his beloved son. But an angel appeared at the last minute, offering a ram for the sacrifice instead of the son. Isaac was spared the knife, and Abraham was spared the unbearable loss. Why was Abraham spared the very thing that this poor widow was now enduring? Perhaps Abraham's righteousness earned him this salvation, whereas the woman's sins denied her any grace at all. Surely a God of grace would not allow a beloved son to die. But she did not have time to think all these thoughts; Elijah acted before she could respond at all.

> Elijah took the boy from her bosom, carried him up to the upper room where he lived, and laid him on his own bed. Elijah cried out to Yahweh, "O Yahweh, my God, have you brought disaster upon the widow with whom I am staying, by killing her son?" Then he stretched himself upon the child three times, and cried out to Yahweh, "O Yahweh, my God, let the life of this child come back into him." Yahweh obeyed the voice of Elijah; the life of the child came back into him, and he lived.
>
> 1 Kings 17:19b–22

Elijah snatched the boy's corpse out of his mother's arms and ran away with it. He took it upstairs to his own room. Hearing this story, an ancient Jew would be horrified. Death was unclean; it separated persons who touched it from their God. God was the God of life and would have nothing to do with death. For a prophet, a man of God, to take hold of this death would be truly horrifying. How can God do any work in the world if God's own people sully themselves with death and uncleanness? The first readers might have thought that if Elijah would have kept his senses and refused to touch the corpse, then God might have been able to work some sort of miracle through the prophet. Although the boy was dead, the mother was still alive, and perhaps food could once again be provided in a miraculous way in order to keep her fed and alive. Some would have said that Elijah should have tended to the living, instead of wasting time on the dying.

Elijah does not fear his own contamination, however. He embraces the dead boy and carries him away. Not only does he touch this corpse, but he brings it into his own room and lays it on his own bed. If this was not enough, he lays down on top of the dead child, not once but three times. Surely this would cause the most serious defilement! But Elijah knows what his critics would never have guessed—that God's miracles can overcome even the presence of death. What follows is hardly the typical pattern for miracles. Elijah does not pray in some gingerly fashion, with the proper positions of humility and tones of trepidation in approaching the seat of the divine. He does not supplicate the deity, begging for favor or for unearned grace. He does not praise God for past acts of grace or for salvation yet to come. Instead, the prophet shouts. He begins with a condemnation of murder, and he points the finger straight at God. Then he shouts a command: "O God, save this child!"

Anyone who reads the Old Testament knows that giving commands is God's business, not anyone else's. Genesis begins when God commands light into existence, and God's commanding continues through the Torah and the Ten Commandments. When God commands, the people listen and obey. Now, however, Elijah commands God to do what had not been done before—to restore life to a dead boy. God listens and obeys; the child lives again. For the first time, at Elijah's command, God brings a child back from death. Death is challenged, and death loses. The son lives!

> Elijah took the child, brought him down from the upper room into the house, and gave him to his mother. Elijah said, "See, your son lives." The woman said to Elijah, "Now I know that you are a man of God. The word of Yahweh is truly in your mouth."
>
> 1 Kings 17:23–24

The end of the story is virtually anticlimactic. The son has been lifted up to the high place of the roof, where God brings life in the face of death; now Elijah brings the living son back down and gives him to the widow, saying, "See? He's alive." Elijah acts as if nothing unusual had ever happened. He claims no credit for the deed. He does not tell how he accused God of murder and commanded God to breathe life into the boy, just as God had breathed life into the first human (Genesis 2:7). It seems not to matter that God had done something not seen since the Garden of Eden. Elijah does not even recount the miracle.

But the widow knows. She knows a miracle has happened. She calls Elijah a "man of God," and in those few words she says so much. She admits her trust of Elijah and her proper thankfulness to him, but beyond that, she confesses her belief in God. She knows that the miracle was God's doing; only God could have done something with that much power and that much care. She had always seen Elijah and respected his work; in the life of her only son, she has seen God.

Jesus and the Widow's Son

Elijah's miracle with the widow's son became the stuff of legends. For this and other deeds, all Israel remembered him as a mighty worker of miracles and as a faithful servant of God. But through the generations, others arose who claimed to have the same divinely granted powers that Elijah possessed. Some of these persons were God's true servants and others were charlatans, but none could compare to Elijah and his miracle of power over death. The coming to earth of one like Elijah was even seen as a sure sign of God's approaching day of wonder and purification (Malachi 4:5). Each new miracle-worker was measured against Elijah, and they were all found wanting. So the centuries passed.

Some eight hundred years after Elijah, another miracle-worker came. Although some thought this one to be a charlatan like so many others, this Jesus never claimed to be much of anything. Actions and sermons did the speaking for him. The Gospel of Luke records a series of miracles that echo the ancient stories about Elijah (Luke 7—8). Jesus had been working in Galilee, but now he had turned south, on a long trek that would eventually lead to Jerusalem. He had already gained a substantial following, and together they were about to enter a town called Nain, on the southern border of Galilee.

> Soon afterward, Jesus entered a town called Nain, and his disciples and a large crowd went with him. As he approached the gate of the town, a man who had died was being carried out. He was his mother's only son, and she was a widow. A large crowd from the town was with her. When the Lord saw her, he had compassion for her and said to her, "Do not weep." Stepping forward, he touched the bier, and the bearers stood still. Jesus said, "Young man, I say to you, rise!" The dead man sat up and started to speak, and Jesus gave him to his mother. Fear seized all of them, and they glorified God, saying, "A great prophet has risen among us!" and "God has looked favorably on the people!" This word about him spread throughout Judea and all the surrounding country.
> Luke 7:11–17

Jesus enters the story of this widow when it is already too late. Unlike Elijah, who knows the widow and cares for her, bringing her life long before the death of her son, Jesus steps into the situation only after death has already visited.

The story begins to move in one direction and then suddenly shifts. At the start, it seems as if this will be a triumphal entry story. Jesus' followers surround him in a joyous throng, having recently witnessed a magnificent healing and still having the words of Jesus' great sermon ringing in their ears. The city gates are right in front of them, and they begin their entry into this city. But then the progression of the story collides head-on with a procession leaving the city. It is a funeral procession, and the large mass of people clogs the narrow city gates. Jesus and his message of life cannot enter; the gates are too full of mourning and death.

Jesus sees and has compassion. This is more than an emotional reaction; it is also a commitment to action. Jesus' words are as brief as Elijah's: "Do not weep." Perhaps the widow misunderstood. Perhaps she had heard of Jesus and of his miracles and teachings. If so, maybe she knew that this was a true miracle-worker, but that no miracles could bring back a dead child. Only Elijah's miracles were that powerful, and Elijah had only been able to resuscitate a child freshly dead. This widow's son had been dead longer; the funeral procession had had time to assemble. Perhaps the widow thought that Jesus was glib: "Don't cry, don't worry. Deny the pain, because pain doesn't do anyone any good. Instead, listen to my message, a message of God's love and care." If she thought such things, then she would have been bitter. What loving, caring God would kill a widow's son?

But she hardly had any time to think such thoughts. Jesus leaves her side in a flash and walks to the bier that carried the corpse. Jesus, rabbi though he was, does not hesitate to touch the unclean bier that carries death, even if it means his own uncleanness. Like Elijah, Jesus is unconcerned by uncleanness. Death and life are matters too serious for any scruples about cleanness and holiness.

Jesus speaks directly to the dead man: "Get up!" The corpse rises and starts talking, fully alive once more, and Jesus helps him down and takes him to his mother. The miracle itself takes such a short time that no one could see it happening before it was over. But when it was done, it stunned everyone around, and the crowd stopped and stared in silence. After this, the mother does not speak at all in this story. That is a great contrast to the Elijah story, where the widow confesses her faith in God by speaking to the prophet. Here, the widow and the living son disappear. The confession is given not just by the people who benefited from Jesus' miracle but by the whole town. They admit its power and assert its glory. They know Jesus is a great prophet, just like Elijah, sent by God to bring life into a dying world. Jesus is a visible expression, a true incarnation, of God's favor for the people. The people see this, confess it, and spread the news throughout the whole countryside.

Luke tells several stories about Jesus that sound like the tales of Elijah (Luke 7—8). Afterward, Jesus prays alone with the disciples, and then asks them, "Who do the crowds say that I am?" (Luke 9:18). Some say John the Baptist, but some even said that Jesus was Elijah. Luke has certainly depicted Jesus in a way that is almost identical to Elijah. To claim that a prophet like Elijah was walking the earth would have been truly remarkable news. Elijah was a prophet with the power to bring life, just like Jesus. Peter, however, utters something that Jesus considers scandalous and orders the disciples not to repeat: Jesus is the Messiah of God. Jesus was like Elijah, and the whole public could see that. But Jesus was even more than that prophet of old, and that knowledge had to be kept secret. Elijah had experienced—and even commanded—God's power over death and life. Jesus had brought life to a widow's son, but his greatest experiences with death were yet to come.

Paul and Eutychus

Jesus was not the last person to bring life to the dead. The apostle Paul found the opportunity at least once. The humorous story should be told in every church throughout the world, as a special celebration of God's life-giving power and goodness.

On the first day after the Sabbath, when we gathered to break bread, Paul was holding a discussion with them. Since he intended to leave on the next day, he extended his speaking until midnight. There were many lamps upstairs where we were gathered. A young man named Eutychus, who was sitting in the window, was overwhelmed by a deep sleep while Paul talked still longer. Overcome by sleep, he fell to the ground three floors below and was picked up dead. Paul went down, bent over him, took him in his arms, and said, "Do not be alarmed, for his life is in him." Then Paul went upstairs, and after he had broken bread and eaten, he continued to converse with them until dawn; then he left. They had taken the boy away alive and were not a little comforted.

Acts 20:7–12

The sermon went on forever. It started over an early supper; more people joined in as the night went on. It would be Paul's last time to talk to these people in Troas, since he and the rest of the group had to leave in the morning. The hours passed and Paul kept talking. It grew dark and people became restless; Paul kept talking. Even around midnight, when people were getting sleepy and beginning to nod off, Paul kept talking. One person could not take it any more. One can hardly blame poor Eutychus; this sermon had gone on some six hours or so, and Paul never claimed to be the most exciting speaker. Moreover, they were meeting in an upstairs room, where it was sure to be hotter even at night, and there were many lamps burning, giving off their heat in the midst of this room full of people. It must have been far too warm to be comfortable. In that heat and at that hour, it would be natural to become drowsy, and perhaps even to doze a little.

It was doubtful that Eutychus was the only one to feel so sleepy, but Eutychus had one noticeable difference: He was sitting in a window. Perhaps he had moved over there a half hour before, when he first started to get sleepy, so that he could get some fresh air and wake himself up. But it didn't work well at all, and after a while he fell sound asleep—and fell right out the window, three stories down to his death.

For the first time in six hours, Paul stopped for a breath and declared a short break. He stretched a bit and then walked down the steps and went outside the building to see what was going on. He saw that Eutychus had already been picked up by some bystanders who had seen this young man drop to his death. There must have been wailing and cries of loss and pain throughout; people up and down the street would have been waking up and lighting lamps to go outside and see what was happening. Paul walked over to the people holding Eutychus' lifeless body, and then he reached out and held Eutychus himself.

As Paul held him, life miraculously reentered Eutychus. Some friends helped him walk away, healed but still a little dazed. Paul went back up to the room and the crowd returned with him. After a midnight snack, Paul settled back into speaking as if nothing had happened. He finished about six hours later, around dawn.

As in all of these stories, there is almost no sense that an earth-shattering miracle has happened in their sight. In this story in Acts, there is no mention at all of faith's increase as a result of witnessing this stupendous event. Instead, the boy walks off, the crowd returns to the room where death had just visited, and Paul eats and keeps talking. Death and life meet in passing, and hardly anyone bats an eyelash.

Lazarus

The Gospel of John tells an amazing story of life's return, set in the dead center of the book (John 11). The writer of this Gospel admits to knowing more stories than he could possibly include, but his Gospel is the only one to contain this miracle story. John's Gospel admits Jesus' special nature in a much more straightforward way than the other Gospels. Whereas Luke records Jesus accepting the title of Messiah (or Christ) but wishing the disciples not to tell, John shows another side. John's Jesus accepts the title Messiah in public, while talking to a hostile group in the temple (John 10:24). These Jews understand Jesus' words as blasphemy, and they threaten to stone him. Jesus narrowly escapes arrest and flees to the other side of the Jordan River, where he seems to be safe for the moment (John 10:39–40).

In that secure isolation, a message comes that Jesus' close friend, Lazarus, was ill. His sisters, Mary and Martha, who were also good friends of Jesus, had sent the message so that Jesus would come. Lazarus lived in one of Jerusalem's outlying suburbs, and Jerusalem was full of people who wanted to see Jesus dead, so Jesus, in that dreamy, far-seeing, prophetic voice that appears throughout John's Gospel, says to the disciples, "Lazarus' illness won't result in death. Instead, it will bring glory to God" (John 11:4). With that, Jesus goes back to his business.

Two days pass, and out of the blue, Jesus tells his disciples, "Let's go near Jerusalem." They think Jesus is crazy; they are convinced that death by stoning is the certain result of a trip to Jerusalem. Jesus tells them not to worry, and after a while, explains in that distant, dreamy voice, "Our friend Lazarus has fallen asleep, but I'll go wake him up" (John 11:11). The disciples never bother to ask Jesus how he knows all of these things, but they argue that there would be no need to visit Lazarus. If the disease has abated enough that he can sleep peacefully, then it will pass soon and he will be fine. Jesus looks down for a minute and an edge creeps into his voice: "Lazarus is dead. I'm glad I wasn't there, so that you can believe. Let's go." Thomas reluctantly agrees: "Let's go too; we'll all die there together" (John 11:14-16).

Elsewhere Thomas may doubt, but here he knows exactly what the score is. Going to Jerusalem is a life and death matter. It means death for Jesus and for all of his disciples. The reason is simple: They believe. Belief leads to death, but it is the kind of death with Jesus that is right to seek. In faith, Jesus and the twelve march straight toward their deaths. Jesus simply reached that goal of death much sooner than the rest. The disciples do not realize how much is truly at stake though. It is a matter of death and life in more ways than they know.

Two more days pass, and Jesus arrives at the outskirts of Bethany, Lazarus' home town. Here the shocking, unsurprising news is given: Lazarus died four days ago, about the time that Jesus received the initial message. Martha leaves the crowds to meet Jesus outside, and she expresses her faith in Jesus' unused and untested, but now irrelevant, abilities: "Had you been here, you could have saved him." Jesus replies, "Your brother will rise again." Martha had heard those simple words of piety so many times before in these last four days. The Pharisees and many of the other Jews believed that on the last day of this present world, all the dead would rise to life. Unfortunately, words of a future day of glory rarely counterbalance the present pain. Martha's emptiness is too great to be filled with statements about a glorious someday that might never come in her own lifetime. What good is a promise that is fulfilled only after death?

Jesus shakes his head for a moment and then explains: "*I am resurrection and life.*" Martha answers in a faithful confession: "I believe that you are the Messiah, the Son of God, the one coming into the world" (John 11:25–27). But all her beliefs are still in the future, where they provide so little comfort. Even after Jesus tells her straightforwardly, Martha still believes that death overcomes life until the end of the age. Death is inevitable, even if life comes after it. Martha thinks on these things as she goes to find her sister, Mary, and bring her to Jesus. Mary's faith causes her to know that Jesus could have healed Lazarus when he was ill, but she too cannot acknowledge that Jesus could trade death for life.

At this point, there is nothing left for Jesus to do but act. He approaches the cavernous tomb while the crowd is watching, aghast. Quietly, he calls for the rock to be moved, for the tomb to be opened. Martha softly mentions the stench of a four-day-old corpse, but Jesus insists and prays to heaven in the hearing of the whole crowd. Then, he raises his voice and shouts, "Get out here, Lazarus!" (John 11:43). And as everyone watches and whispers, the dead arises and walks on the earth once more.

Suddenly the scene shifts to council chambers, where the Pharisees, the Sadducees, and other prominent persons of faith meet. They argue that they cannot let these things continue; the people will get too excited. High Priest Caiaphas insists that the needs of the many outweigh the life of one person. They establish firm plans to remove the threatening Jesus. As crowds celebrated Lazarus' life in Bethany, councils plan Jesus' death in Jerusalem. This was truly a matter of death and life. For the first time in all these stories of new life, we begin to realize how great the cost might be.

John's Beheading

Others had already discovered the cost of dealing with death and life. John the Baptist had preached life, a new kind of life that energized the people who heard him. No one fell asleep during John's powerful sermons. There was some opposition, but John always seemed to handle it well, and no one lingered around to bother John all that much. The Gospels do not tell much of John's story, but one flashback scene occurs after Herod the ruler begins to think that Jesus might be John, resurrected:

Herod had seized John, bound him, and put him in prison on account of Herodias, his brother Philip's wife, because John had been telling him, "It is not permitted for you to have her." Though Herod wanted to kill him, he feared the crowd, because they thought of him as a prophet. But when Herod's birthday came, Herodias' daughter danced before the company, and she pleased Herod so much that he promised on oath to grant her whatever she might ask. Prompted by her mother, she said, "Give me the head of John the Baptist here on a platter, I ask." The king was grieved, yet out of regard for his oaths and for the guests, he commanded it to be given. He sent and had John beheaded in the prison.

John's head was brought on a platter and given to the girl, who took it to her mother. His disciples came and took the body and buried it. Then, they went and told Jesus.

Matthew 14:3–12

John had preached life; Herod visited death upon him. John ate a simple diet of locusts and honey; his head became a great feast's centerpiece and trophy. For such a serious person, it seems a tragically trivial death. But even such a grotesque, absurd death can point to meaning. His death enters into the permanent record of human history because he was martyred for his belief. His stand for morality in government was powerful, and the rulers of this world demanded a price for that strong voice. Persons of faith hear the tale of John's faith and commitment, and even today courage arises to oppose the powers-that-be in the cause of righteousness. Such stands carry a price; but the remembered and empowering death of a martyr is a death that brings life to a new generation.

Stephen's Martyrdom

John the Baptist was hardly the last martyr of the faith. In its earliest days, the church realized the needs brought by hunger and poverty. To combat these problems, the whole church selected seven servants who would dedicate themselves to feeding the poor on a daily basis (Acts 6:1–6). Of these seven, the best known was Stephen. Stephen was strong in his service and that loyalty made him some enemies. These opponents took exception with the new emphases that Stephen and the other Christians were making and they wished to stop Stephen from continuing his work. Such was not an easy task; Stephen's dedication was legendary. The enemies plotted, and they brought Stephen before the court to be judged on false charges. When given the opportunity to defend himself, Stephen seized the moment to preach about Jesus Christ. At that point, the crowd turned ugly.

When they heard these things, they became enraged in their hearts and they ground their teeth at Stephen. But filled with the Holy Spirit, Stephen gazed into heaven and saw the glory of God and Jesus standing at the right hand of God. He said, "Look! I see the heavens opened and the

Son of Man standing at the right hand of God!" With a loud shout, they covered their ears and rushed together against him. They dragged him out of the city and began to stone him. (The witnesses laid their coats at the feet of a young man named Saul.) While they were stoning Stephen, he prayed, "Lord Jesus, receive my spirit." Kneeling down, he cried out in a loud voice, "Lord, do not hold this sin against them." When he had said this, he died.

Acts 7:54–60

Like Elijah, Stephen served God by feeding the poor. He brought life to the impoverished and the disadvantaged by providing them nourishment. Feeding the poor is a matter of death and life. Like John the Baptist, Stephen's commitment to a call and a task carried with it a price. The one who brought life received death as payment for his labors.

The world fought against those who would bring life and threatened to take their life away. But at the end, Stephen asserted his faith once more. He prayed that Jesus take his life. The nonbelievers had no right to take Stephen's life; such life belonged only to God. Stephen had committed his living to the path of Jesus before the stones started to fly; it was just one more step to commit his dying as well.

But the book of Acts sneaks in an unexpected sentence. Saul was there, watching it all happen. Saul does not reappear for a while more, when he was converted after a noteworthy career of persecuting Christians. Almost without noticing, the trade of death and life continued. Stephen gave life to the starving and received death in turn. Saul witnesses death and, before long, becomes truly alive.

Last Supper

Communion itself remembers death and life. When we partake of the elements in memory of Jesus, it is right to remember both Jesus' life, full of teachings and signs, and Jesus' death, which is no less full of meaning. Communion's very roots delve into the thin space between life and death.

Communion celebrates life, because it is full of life itself. Jesus' whole life climaxes with that one first communion where all the truth is placed on the table. Food is for the living, and this food contains the very essence of life. But death is also at the table. The church's first communion is Jesus' last supper. The bread and the wine at that Passover meal predicted and symbolized Jesus' coming death. When Jesus identified the bread and the cup, he referred to the *broken* body and the *poured-out* blood of a Jesus who died. So the elements today remind us of death—Jesus' death, the martyr's death, our death.

Communion embodies and embraces both death and life. It combines both because it has the power to break the boundary between them. In human experience, the utter difference between death and life seems inviolable and inevitable, but when God moves through the world such distinctions can be broken. Death and life were broken when Elijah commanded God to bring life to a widow's dead son, when Jesus brought life to another widow's dead son at Nain, when Paul held and resuscitated the fatally drowsy Eutychus, and when Jesus called Lazarus to come out of the cave. Death and life were broken when John's death brought life to Jesus' witness and when Stephen's martyrdom brought life to Saul and to the church's commitment to feeding the hungry. Death and life were broken when Jesus' death on the cross echoed life through all time and space. At that moment when Jesus died, the graves all around sprang open and the dead rejoined the living (Matthew 27:52–53). The saints and poets sang, "Death, where is your sting?" (1 Corinthians 15:55; see Hosea 13:14).

Each time the church joins in communion, the bread and the cup break death and life, bringing the two together. The first communion took place in an upper room just like those upper rooms where Elijah and Paul held sons and crossed the line between death and life. The communion meal became the place where Jesus could be seen alive, even after death. Luke tells about those who saw the resurrected Jesus on the road to Emmaus, but did not recognize him until they saw the bread broken (Luke 24:30–35). John tells of Jesus' disciples, who meet the resurrected Jesus early in the morning on their way to go fishing, and they do not recognize Jesus until he serves them breakfast. Jesus hosts the table today; there the crucified Messiah can be seen alive. Communion breaks down the boundaries between death and life.

Where life and death are mingled, they are both granted. Meaningful life and meaningful death both belonged to the Jesus of the communion table, and at that table Jesus offers the same meaning to us. We are left at communion with the power of life and death. This power and this love combine in bread and cup. In remembrance of Jesus' life, death, and resurrection, and in remembrance of all the other lives and deaths in past and in future, the bread and the cup are before us, offering a choice.

> See, I place before you today life and prosperity, death and disaster, since I am commanding you today to love Yahweh your God, to walk in God's ways, and to observe God's commandments, decrees, and ordinances, so you can live and become numerous, and Yahweh your God will bless you in the land that you are entering to possess. But if your heart turns away and you do not hear, but are led astray, bowing down to other gods and serving them, I declare to you today that you shall utterly perish; you will not prolong your days in the land that you are crossing the Jordan to enter and possess. Today, I call heaven and earth to witness against you that I place before you life and death, blessings and curses. Choose life so that you and your descendants may live, by loving Yahweh your God, by obeying God, and by clinging to God. This is your life and the length of your days, to dwell in the land that Yahweh swore to give to your ancestors, to Abraham, to Isaac, and to Jacob.
>
> Deuteronomy 30:15–20

This old call to faith echoes into communion. Life and death are mingled in the cup; blessing and cursing both lie in our possible futures. The bread and cup of blessing, full of life and death, are ours to eat and drink, but it depends on our choice. The remembrance of our ancestors in the faith reverberates around us, encouraging our right choice, and God sits down to the table, inviting us to join with all who have lived and all who have died. The bread and cup bring meaning both to living and to dying, because they bring Jesus' death to those who live and Jesus' life to those who die. Death and life are mingled here and all the boundaries, even the boundaries between God and humanity, disappear.

11

conclusion

Communion is many things to many people. It is a meal, a covenant, a sacrament, and so much more. If this book has done nothing else, then perhaps it has broadened the notions of what communion is. Communion is Jesus' body and blood. It is the middle of worship or the climax of worship. It is daily, weekly, monthly, quarterly, or once in a lifetime. It is priestly, pastoral, prophetic, comforting, challenging, encouraging, shocking. It belongs to God on high; it belongs to the basest of persons. Communion is an ancient sacrifice, manna from heaven, a Passover meal, a cleansing, a commitment, a cup of grace, a cup of wrath, death, life, meaning for death and life, atonement, covenant, restriction, freedom, morality, diversity, unity; it is bread and wine, God and people.

More than anything else, communion is a meeting place. It is where all of these notions come together and somehow co-exist. Communion is where humans meet each other, so it is in a sense where the church is born out of the many individuals who arrive. At the table God and humanity sit down across from each other for common purposes. And it all begins with bread and wine.

When the elements come together, they unite many of the different ideas that they symbolize. Bread can mean so many things. It is the staff of life, the symbol of sustenance. It is provision and grace. It is sufficient manna. Wine is potent, powerful, changing. It is dark and dangerous. Wine intoxicates and befuddles; God's cup challenges and transforms. It is

Passover's cup of blessing and God's cup of wrath.

When the people come together, they become church. Individuals may gather there, but the table takes those separate persons and molds them together into something greater than the sum of the parts, without violating selfhood. Community is more than being in the same room. The communion table allows common purpose and common identity to take hold in the lives of those around. As church, this community gains new sensitivities. We begin to understand the joy that should be ours because of our new identity as God's people. We realize that worship is celebration and that togetherness is a party. Life with God is fun!

We also realize how serious it is. We strive to make sure that all will hear the invitation that God announces, and that nothing will stand in their way. We work to remove the stumbling blocks of poverty, racism, sexism, nationalism, and oppression, along with all the other ways that humanity divides itself against itself. No separations can be allowed because all should come together as equals at God's table. Together, the church realizes how great the need for morality is. We become distinctively God's own people at this table, and we cease to accept all the world's values. God gives new meanings to our lives and to our common life. The table makes us God's people, and then it makes us God's peculiar, chosen, distinct people.

When God and people come together at the table, the partnership moves into action. We have become church and we have become God's partners in the tasks that God values. We enter into covenant with God to undertake the transformation of the world. When sin blocks this transformation, we work together with God to eradicate it. God will stop at nothing to save the world, and in partnership with God we have the same dedication to the task. Not even death can serve as a boundary, because God is truly unstoppable. Although there are setbacks and times when we need God's soothing grace to reempower us for the ever-continuing task, God's work is unceasing and the ultimate success is assured. Within this partnership, both life and death have meaning, as the table of communion commemorates.

When Old and New Testaments come together in the church's worship, new possibilities emerge. Ancient wine in new wineskins is potent. Renewal is waiting to happen when all of these Old Testament images are allowed to transform our worship. Worship, like all of our faith, needs to be grounded firmly in all the Bible. Such combinations of biblical images further the praise of God. They allow the expression of our diversity, because of the many available themes. At the same time, a deeper unity resides, because it is one God whom we worship.

Communion is a rich feast. It gains its richness from the God who presides at the table and also from the many ways of knowing God that unite there. Within that great wealth of knowledge and relationship are more than ideas. There are fresh possibilities for worship and life. At the table we come together to meet our common God and to join in unity with God in our common work. Each time we drink the cup and eat the bread, let us do so in remembrance of all the ways in which God calls us to that partnership.

index of scriptures